GET PUBLISHED!
GET PRODUCED!

Tips On How To Sell Your Writing from America's #1 Literary Agent

PETER MILLER

lone eagle
PUBLISHING COMPANY

Los Angeles, CA

LONE EAGLE PUBLISHING CO., LLC™
2337 Roscomare Road, Suite Nine
Los Angeles, CA 90077-1851
Phone: 800-FILMBKS • Toll Free Fax: 888-FILMBKS
www.loneeagle.com & www.eaglei.com

Printed in the United States of America
Cover and book design by Blake Busby
Cover photo by Loren Haynes

Parts of Appendix A, B and C were used with permission
from the following copyrighted works.
Accidental Millionaire. © 1987 by Lee Butcher.
Fatal Freeway. © 1987 by Steve Salerno.
Hollywood's Golden Year: 1939. © 1988 by Ted Sennett.
New Orleans Creole Cookery. © 1989 by Bookman, Inc.
How To Write And Give A Speech. © 1982 by Joan Detz.
Spontaneous Remissions. © 1988 by Albert Marchetti, M.D.
The Killer's Game. © 1996 by Jay R. Bonansinga
The Jersey Devil. © 1987 by Christopher Cook Gilmore
True Murder Mysteries. © 1987 by Bugliosi Enterprises, Inc. /
    The Peter Miller Agency, Inc.
True Murder Mysteries. © 1988 by Bugliosi Enterprises, Inc. /
    The Peter Miller Agency, Inc.
The Inside Man. © 1990 by Jerry Schmetterer.

Library of Congress Cataloging-in-Publication Data

Miller, Peter
     Get published! Get produced! : tips on how to sell your writing from America's #1 literary agent / by Peter Miller.
         p.   cm.
     ISBN 0-943728-73-8
     ISBN 0-943728-92-4 (pbk.)
     1. Authorship—Marketing.   I. Title.
     PN161.M55   1997
     808'.02—dc21   97-23131
                                                 CIP

Lone Eagle Publishing Company is a registered trademark.

DEDICATION

This book is dedicated to my wife Giselle
and daughters Liseanne and Margo
who taught be something more important
than how to get published and produced,
how to love.

CONTENTS

Dedication v

Acknowledgments ix

Foreword xi

Preface xvii

Introduction 1

Chapter One
PROTOCOL 11

Chapter Two
NONFICTION 17

Chapter Three
FICTION 29

Chapter Four
WONDERFUL CIRCUMSTANCES 43

Chapter Five
SPECIALTY BOOKS 51

Chapter Six
HOW TO SELL YOUR WRITING
FOR FEATURE FILMS OR TELEVISION 55

Chapter Seven
PACKAGING 75

Chapter Eight
MARKETING YOUR SCREENPLAY 85

Chapter Nine
THE EPISODIC TELEVISION SERIES 93

<u>Chapter Ten</u>
CONTRACTS 99

    Sample Short-form Deal Memo 107

<u>Appendix A</u>
THE NONFICTION BOOK PROPOSAL

    1. The Accidental Millionaire 115

    2. Fatal Freeway 153

    3. Hollywood's Goldenyear, 1939 175

    4. New Orleans Creole Cookery 185

    5. How To Write And Give A Speech 197

    6. Spontaneous Remissions/Beating The Odds 203

FORMATTING / STYLE SAMPLE
    The Killer's Game 225

<u>Appendix B</u>
THE FICTION PROPOSAL

    The Jersey Devil 231

<u>Appendix C</u>
THE TELEVISION SERIES PROPOSAL

    1. True Murder Mysteries 239

    2. The Inside Man 271

<u>Appendix D</u>
THE NOVEL COVERAGE 293

ACKNOWLEDGMENTS

I'd like to extend a special thanks to all the friends, colleagues and clients who helped me develop and write this book, beginning with my original editor David Weaver; my new editor, Michelle Manafy; my former associate Helen Pfeffer; my company's vice president and director of development, Jennifer Robinson; and my associate Yuri Skujins.

I also want to thank my publishers, Joan and Ralph Singleton, for having the foresight to see the need for this book; Jeff Black, my new wizard in publishing; Blake Busby for his kind patience; and Lone Eagle for blessing me with Janna Wong Healy's editorial input; and also to my friends and clients, who gave me the right to use their proposals in this book, including Jay Bonansigna, Vincent Bugliosi; Lee Butcher; Joan Detz; Christopher Cook Gilmore; Roy Guste; Albert Marchetti, M.D.; Steve Salerno; Jerry Schmetterer and Ted Sennett, and all of the authors who have given me the honor of being their literary manager over the years.

I'd like to give a special thanks to my friend and business associate, Jon Karas, for giving me the vision to have the original book republished. Also, a special thanks to Mr. Jay Bonansigna, the Italian god of contemporary authors, for his wonderful foreword and his belief in me. Keep an eye on this Bonansigna name—this man oozes with talent.

FOREWORD

Peter Miller saved my life.

Let me reiterate for good measure: Peter the Great—literary lion, rider of the purple page, peerless pitbull of professional prose—saved my proverbial butt. OK, maybe he didn't drag me out of a burning building or dive on a hand grenade or loan me a kidney, but still, Peter Miller saved me from certain doom as surely as a paramedic applying CPR to my miserable own self.

Flashback to 1991. I was naive, vulnerable, self-absorbed film school graduate wallowing in the after-stench of a stalled first feature. The details of my downfall aren't important; although the broad strokes were all-too familiar. After winning some festival awards for my thesis film, I figured I'd slip on my beret and jodhpurs and pull a "Citizen Kane." I would direct a major motion picture with local talent in Chicago. Next stop, Quentin Tarantino-ville. But of course, it doesn't work like that. In the real world, there are no such things as people like Quentin Tarantino. Or Orson Welles. Or Santa Claus. In the real world, there are only first films that fall apart faster than a marriage proposal from David Lee Roth.

After the dust settled, I hit rock bottom. In fact, I fell through the bottom, penetrating the earth's crust and landing somewhere a few miles south of China. To paraphrase Josh White, I was so far down, it was all starting to look like up to me. My directing career was stalled, my other screenplays were stalled, my life was stalled. Months of antidepressants and Double-Stuff Oreos followed. Other than a few short stories published in a few outré quarterlies, I was strictly S-O-L.

Then I ran across a listing in the "Agency" section of the *Writer's Digest Writer's Guide.*

There was something about the PMA Literary and Film Management Company that sank a hook into me. Led by a boyish-looking Tasmanian devil named Peter Miller, the company came off as small, yet sophisticated; intimate, yet global; intelligent, yet aggressive; and maybe most importantly for me, active on both coasts, representing writing talent in both media—literature and film. Suddenly, I had this weird epiphany: If I could hook my wagon to somebody like Peter, I could avoid being so damn vulnerable.

I quickly sent off a couple of manuscripts—a screenplay and a first draft of a first novel, if I remember correctly—and then waited suicidally by the telephone. The rejection letter came exactly two weeks later. But—and this is a colossal "but"—the manner in which Peter rejected me was so damned encouraging, I decided to keep pursuing him. Which brings me to the first reason Peter Miller is so darned handy.

PROFESSIONALISM

After getting the brush-off, I called Mister "M" and begged him to let me rewrite, especially since his in-house development guru—Jennifer "The Literary Goddess" Robinson— had been so complimentary in the kiss-off letter.

From that moment on, Peter was a consummate pro. He agreed to look at a rewrite, and furthermore, he provided an in-depth evaluation of my screenplay to help me. I went back to work with the intensity of a monk on Methadone. In a month or so, I had the script revised and polished. When I sent it back in, Peter was suitably impressed, but not yet convinced. See, the essence of this guy is very simple: He's only interested in Results with a capital R, and he knows he cannot get results until the product is letter perfect.

By now, I was happy to continue rewriting. I had finally found an ally. An advisor. A protector. A big, beautiful, inflatable life-preserver tossed around me. I threw away the Prozac and stocked up on long-grain mimeo and computer discs. After a third and final draft of the screenplay, I finally signed on with PMA.

Which leads me to another faced of Peter that makes him so indispensable.

A RELENTLESS PURSUIT OF SUCCESS

If you're reading this book, I probably don't have to tell you that the publishing and movie businesses are about as cutthroat and competitive as the bullet-proof vest concessions in Beirut. In a typical week, for instance, a Hollywood studio receives over a hundred book manuscripts for consideration. Needless to say, my little "spec" screenplay was not an easy sell. I had no track record, no Hollywood credits, no power, no table at Spago. But dammit, I had Peter Miller in my corner and Peter is absolutely relentless.

One of the best things Peter did for me was begin to market me—in his inimitable sales lingo—as a "triple threat." In other words, he began to position me as a novelist-screenwriter-film maker. This rather pretentious hyphenate did more than merely focus my identity in the marketplace, it convinced me to self-fulfill this prophecy. I started writing down my movie ideas as novels and I started adapting my own fiction as screenplays, and Peter started making waves in the wacky biz we call show.

Which reminds me of another reason a struggling writer should pay very close attention to what Peter says.

CONNECTIONS AND CREATIVITY

Peter Miller not only knows how to recognize and shape a commercial piece of fiction, he knows where to go to get it sold. This may sound obvious, but there's more to Peter Miller's success than simple "agenting." Peter is the Jake LaMotta of literary managers: He takes a licking and keeps on ticking. His connections are innumerable, but his energy is far greater.

Take my first novel, *The Black Mariah*, for instance. Ostensibly a horror novel, it was completed in the fall of 1992, a time when the genre of supernatural horror had reached an all time—commercially at least. The sad fact was, unless you had a last name that began with a "K"—such as King or Koontz —you were relegated to the bottom of the paperback spinner at your local bus depot. But Peter Miller saw a lot more potential in my little tale of itinerant truck drivers who are infected with an ancient curse. Peter helped me shape the book into a fast-paced thriller with major movie potential. And by the time we got around to sending the manuscript out, we landed three bids from three separate publishers in less than two weeks. I eventually got a deal that was very respectable, even for a mainstream first novel.

But Peter didn't stop there.

Within another month, we had optioned *The Black Mariah* to New Line Cinema for very decent money, and had even managed to attach little ol' me as a screenwriter on the project. Eventually, they signed one of my childhood heroes—George Romero—to direct the film, and I was in hog heaven. The biggest irony was, I had written a novel in order to finally break into the film biz.

But Peter didn't stop there.

Working through a global network of contacts, publishers and sub-rights people, Peter started selling my books around the world. As of this printing, my first three novels have been translated into ten different languages. And not only is this a marvelous, heady experience, but it also allows me to be a full time hyphenate. Praise God. Hallelujah! Pass the royalties! Peter Miller saved me, saved me from the pits of despair. And I was finally made a believer, a born again Miller-phile.

But Peter didn't stop there.

Peter never stops.

Pay close attention to this guy.

Read his book.

The life Peter saves may be your own.

Jay Bonansigna
Evanston, Illinois
Spring 1997

"There's no bigger thrill than telling an author I've just found a publishing home for their book!"

—*PM*

PREFACE

"Writers aren't exactly people...they're a whole lot of people trying to be one person."
—F. Scott Fitzgerald

WRITERS . . . WRITE ON!

Some Nuts-and-Bolts Advice About Getting Published

I have been a literary representative since 1973, almost twenty-five years, and during my years in the publishing business, I've represented numerous authors and placed hundreds of books throughout the world (at last count, over 800). My first-hand experience with the ups and downs of the publishing world has left me with one constant: my admiration for those with the genius, stamina and determination to select writing as a profession. We are regularly told of the willpower and self-sacrifice needed to succeed in other professions, but I say: Try writing a book!

Nothing challenges the mind, sparks the imagination or requires more discipline than writing. If you're a writer, this may seem obvious. But, too often, the basic element of writing—hard work—is forgotten during the hot pursuit of illusory success formulas.

Next to actually writing the book, the greatest problem any writer faces is getting the book published. Every writer who is serious about his profession faces this situation no matter what type of writing he undertakes and regardless of the quality of his work. While I empathize with the writer's anxiety, a lack of objectivity can be self-destructive at the worst possible time—when he or she faces a deadline. As a representative, it is my responsibility to keep the often harsh reality of the publishing industry in sight and to make sure the writer gets published.

The current literary marketplace is so glutted with submissions that a new or struggling writer—even with a good idea or a promising manuscript—has less chance of getting published than ever before. The number of publishers is shrinking, hence, there are fewer buyers. For example, as a result of corporate takeovers and mergers, Doubleday and then Bantam were sold, creating the conglomerate of Bantam Doubleday Dell which is now owned by Bertelsmann of Germany; Viking Penguin acquired NAL; Dutton is now part of Penguin, U.S.A. and The Penguin Group Worldwide acquired The Putnam Berkley Publishing Group; Time, Inc. merged with Warner Communications, making it the largest entertainment company in the world . . . until Disney bought ABC. The publicity received by well-known, best-selling writers, such as James Michener, Stephen King, Tom Clancy, Mary Higgins Clark and Patricia Cornwell, is phenomenal, but the promise of quick success and easy money is an illusion to all other writers. You must be most concerned about your own writing—not the success of other writers. Every author has his own problems and every book is unique, especially when dealing with the marketplace.

I'd like to share five Common Knowledge Recommendations that are designed to help you get published.

1. **Have Faith in Yourself.** This is not as simple as it sounds. Being a writer doesn't end when you've finished typing your manuscript! You may feel confident now, but what happens after a few rejections or some negative criticism? How committed will you be to your writing after your mother and your clos-

est friends give up on you? Can you stand to see your writing friends forge ahead while you're stuck getting writer's cramp? It's important to have confidence enough to complete your manuscript, but it's even more vital to have faith in it when you're ready to let someone read it, or when—on that fateful day—you're ready to submit it to a publisher.

Many of the books I've represented were submitted to a dozen or more publishers and were rejected by all of them. To use a simple analogy, the results of those first innings did not make the whole ball game. The first novel by one of my clients had been turned down by another representative before the client was introduced to me. Two weeks later, I sold his book, in a six-figure sale, to a major U.S. publisher and later placed the rights in Germany, the U.K., Japan, Holland, Korea, Italy and Bulgaria. The author, Michael Eberhardt, is still my client and we recently placed his third novel, *The Fifth Canon*, with Dutton.

About eighteen years ago, I took on a new client, an Australian writer named Roland Perry, who submitted an intriguing first novel to me, Program for a Puppet. *The novel dealt with industrial espionage and the manipulation of the American political scene. What clinched my enthusiasm for it was Perry's belief in his work and his willingness to hang in there for the long haul. I decided to hold my first literary auction. Simultaneously, I submitted the book to fourteen publishers, asking them to read the manuscript in two weeks and to come back to us with an offer of not less than $50,000. I had a nibble from one of the publishers, but it wasn't above my established "floor bid." I was shocked! It was like throwing a party and* *having no one show up! I met with Perry and one of my associates to plot our next strategy. Roland did not lose heart; in fact, he set about editing and fine-tuning the manuscript. His resolve encouraged me: I redoubled my efforts to place his book.*

A month later or so later, I was in London. Of the various projects I considered presenting to the group of British publishers I know, none seemed more deserving than Program for a Puppet. *I submitted the revised manuscript to an English publisher and, happily, it was accepted. It was a case of the right publisher at the right time. Soon after, I arranged for the author to co-write a screenplay based on his novel. Having garnered one publishing agreement, I used that foundation to auction off the American rights to the book. The novel was published in the U.S., Italy, Germany, Spain, Mexico and Japan— in hardback and paperback. The author's faith in himself and his writing, which directly affected my belief in him, paid off. We won!*

2. **Know Your Agent.** Make sure your agent or representative is working FOR you and FOR the success of your book(s), but that doesn't mean your representative should be your buddy: well-meaning friends can hand out bad advice. You should have a good rapport with whomever represents you; you want to feel that you and your agent are playing on the same team and that you're both out to win. It may be worth a trip to New York (the publishing center of the United States) to meet your representative. After all, your choice of representation may be the single, most important decision you make in transforming what was an *avocation* into a *vocation*. And, don't be afraid to question your representative

about all aspects of the business, because he should have the answers.

Working closely with your representative means that both of you should be willing to listen to each other. (If you're the star quarterback of the football team, then your representative is the coach.) Listen to your coach. Your agent shouldn't try to force you to do anything to your book that violates your writing integrity. However, your representative also can't change the realities of the publishing world. (It is very important for you to remember that any move a representative makes on behalf of your book is subject to your final written approval.) It's a representative's business to know what is marketable and what isn't.

If you have experience dealing with the publishing world, my comments may appear overly simplified. However, this recommendation is crucial to any writer who is trying to develop a professional attitude. And, it serves as a reminder that a representative DOES do more for his client than collect a commission.

One of my clients, at work on his second book, was dissatisfied with the way his first book (about the psychology of the stock market) was promoted by its publisher. After his hard work, the first book had been published in hardcover and had sold about 35,000 copies, an excellent number from my estimation. However, his frustration made him angry with me AND the publishing process. In fact, he threatened to quit writing. I explained to him how foolish this threat was: the market definitely would support the book he was planning to write. I convinced him to write a three-page outline for the second book and, *reluctantly, he did so. He later gave his consent when I wanted to submit his proposal to a different publisher. The brief outline, along with his previous book, were presented to one of the most important men in the publishing industry. He bought the proposal, paying a handsome five-figure advance for it. Of course, the author was delighted and immediately began to work on a proposal for a third book. The author is now one of the most successful investment bankers in the country; his once privately-held company recently merged with a large firm that manages almost $5 billion in investment funds. He attributes much of his success to the publicity he received from his books. He has just completed a third book which will be published by the biggest publisher in the world in the Spring of 1998.*

3. **Know the Market.** Publishers want books that sell—period—and there are many elements that contribute to the commercial viability of a book. Therefore, know and accept the CURRENT conditions of the literary marketplace. Read magazines written for writers, such as *Writer's Digest* or *Publishers Weekly*, to get an idea of what publishers are looking for. This doesn't mean you must conform to publishers' expectations but, if you want to succeed, either by their terms or by breaking the rules, you first must know those rules. You might want to explore category (genre) fiction, i.e., horror, romance, western, mystery, etc., which is a good way to begin a career in fiction writing because there is usually a market for it. Or, you might want to write "The Great American Novel."

When I read manuscripts, I always look for a solid plot, substantive, larger-than-life characters and a tight writing style. One characteristic of all novels I've successfully placed is a fast pace, or what the industry calls a "page turner" or "compelling writing." However, the success of any book boils down to one factor: everyone likes a good read. Any editor at any publishing company must read an incredible amount in an abnormally short period of time. Therefore, a book that is slow or poorly written or is presented in a substandard way or is deficient in the basics is not going to attract an editor's attention; it will be rejected faster than you can say, "No."

Editors are dedicated and extremely individualistic people and most have very specific taste. Agents who understand this will be able to help their clients. For example, I have spent a great deal of time developing solid relationships with and nurturing the interests of editors. I can say without a doubt that a representative CAN make the difference between his author getting published and being rejected. Often, an editor relies on an agent's endorsement of an author's credibility: the representative offers his reputation as a form of "collateral." Publishing has always been called a "gentleman's business," and in many ways it still operates this way. A representative's integrity is valuable, but only when coupled with a suitably professional manuscript.

Many publishers today use the committee system to make decisions. Therefore, an enthusiastic editor becomes an absolute necessity. (In many publishing houses, it is necessary for an editor to have the support of several other editors for a positive decision.) Once an editor is hooked, the publishing process begins. You've sold your work! The publisher has literally "sold itself" on your book.

In my pursuit of editors, I've taken a new and rather unusual approach with some projects, particularly novels. Usually, editors require complete novels—a MUST for a first-time author—before making a judgment. Let's say I represent a novel that is reasonably complete. The author and I develop a proposal that consists of the first three to six chapters, as well as a good synopsis of the entire piece. I submit this proposal to editors. The editor is now faced with a far less formidable reading burden and I can anticipate a quicker and more flexible response. If the answer is favorable, we proceed to an evaluation of the entire manuscript, or even to the negotiation of a contract based on the proposal. If the answer is not favorable, we are still in a position to incorporate the editor's suggestions into the manuscript. This allows the author to make a second attempt to sell the book to that editor.

Nonfiction proposals often sell this way because the book is usually dependent on its subject matter for quality rather than on the author's story-telling abilities or writing style. The author researches the subject, writes a brief synopsis (including an Introduction, Preface and/or Foreword, and a Table of Contents) and attaches a few chapters for evaluation (Note: more details on this are found in Chapter Two). If the author has published before, a book proposal on an interesting subject can be placed for an advance with relative ease.

4. **Present Perfect Manuscripts**. Although this recommendation seems obvious, I am amazed at the number of sloppy, unprofessionally presented manuscripts I still receive. Aspiring authors, please note: *messy manuscripts do not become books!* Whenever you prepare a manuscript for submission, it should look as professional as possible. An editor will never get

past the first few pages if a manuscript isn't in perfect shape—and I do mean PERFECT.

This concept may seem out of style after hearing about assiduous editors plucking literary geniuses from the proverbial scrapheap. However, with the advent of the computer and the huge number of unpublished manuscripts that go along with this new technology, editors are now forced to be more selective. A manuscript's presentation is obviously the easiest element of a manuscript to judge.

All proposals and manuscripts should:

- have (at least) one-inch margins;
- be double-spaced;
- be left-justified;
- be typed in a Pica font (such as Courier, 12-point size on a computer, 10 pitch on a typewriter);
- be free of typographical errors;
- be printed on a high quality printer (dot matrix printers are difficult to read); and,
- come enclosed in a sturdy manuscript box. (Photocopied versions must have dark and legible print.)

I will not represent or submit a work unless it is in impeccable condition. Take the time to present your project in the best possible manner and avoid the saddest fate in publishing—an UNNECESSARY rejection. Although computers are a great asset to authors, bear in mind that your manuscript should be presented simply, not riddled with different typefaces like the recent books by Howard Stern or Dennis Rodman. (These are specifically designed—by the publisher—to appeal to a certain market demographic.) (See Appendix A, No. 7.)

5. **Your Script Could Be A Book**. I'd like to take you on a trip to Hollywood. This imaginary journey begins when a new, untested writer comes to me, thinking he has just written the next *Jurassic Park*. After taking the initiative to write the screenplay, he comes to me, convinced that he's a shoo-in for an Academy Award. At this point, I must bring everything crashing down to Earth with my last bit of advice: it doesn't happen like it does in the movies.

   If the publishing world is a jungle, then the film world is a jungle on another planet. Whatever the script's merits, the "political" nature of the film industry versus the cost to make a film makes ANY sale a highly complicated affair . . . and this happens to great screenwriters with regularity. So, a screenplay by an unknown writer is next to impossible to sell.

   In my experience, the key to success in the film industry is *packaging*, i.e., associating "proven" elements with an original, untested product. Ideally, packaging would mean the combination of a best-selling book, a well-known screenwriter, a recognized and successful director and bankable stars. Without all of the elements (or at least one major one), the packager might attempt to option or sell the property by obtaining a star's interest in the screenplay and then by capitalizing on that star's power. This act would move a project into "development."

   Although an unknown writer has little chance of attracting the interest of established people in the film industry, nevertheless, I try to develop ways of giving this aspiring screenwriter a chance at fulfilling his dreams. My strongest piece of advice is to turn a screenplay into a novel. If it's a good script, I'll ask the author to flesh out a few chapters and develop a proposal for the novel. Then, if I really believe in the writer and the project, I'll submit everything (the chapters, proposal and the original screenplay) to an editor. This demonstrates the validity of the project as a book and illustrates the obvious potential it has to become a film. Christopher Cook Gilmore's first novel, *Atlantic City Proof,* was adapted from his own screenplay. I hired him to write the book (making this project my first attempt at packaging). I sent the screenplay and the first three chapters of the novel to eighteen publishers. We received a dozen rejections, but six publishers wanted to buy it! I placed *Atlantic City Proof* with the original proposal. It was fairly successful for a first novel and has been reprinted twice in paperback. I'm STILL trying to make the movie (I've been working on it for almost twenty years), but I'm not giving up because I believe in it. My mother, who once owned an antique furniture store, gave me two wise bits of advice that I always remember. One was, "We can sell anything; we just give it time." The second was, "Son, there's a buyer for everything." Consequently, *Atlantic City Proof* was recently with Aviator Pictures, a movie company owned by famed *ER* star Anthony Edwards (he portrays Dr. Mark Greene), who loves it. We were hoping that, with his endorsement, we'd interest Dreamworks SKG, (the company co-owned by Steven Spielberg, Jeffrey Katzenberg and David Geffen, that produces *ER*) we are still trying.

Editors are sometimes wary of the "film angle" approach. It seems that, today, almost every novel is presented as having a potentially hot movie deal attached to it when, in reality, only a handful of the thousands of published novels ever get made into films. A completed screenplay DOES enhance a proposal because it helps demonstrate the author's commitment to the project. I believe that, in some cases, the extra commitment often makes a difference in placing a book successfully.

Every author wants the biggest possible financial commitment from the best possible publisher. And, every author AND his representative want that publisher to promote the book as heavily as possible. Most writers know that books can die if every aspect of their publication, especially promotion, is not coordinated carefully and pursued aggressively. Currently, there are over 100,000 new books published in the U.S. every year, so competition is fierce. It's not just about writing a good book; this book must also be advertised and promoted like hell!

So, what can you do? Why not gamble on yourself and your work?

Look at *The Thorn Birds,* a second novel by Colleen McCullough, at the time a virtually unknown Australian writer; over fifteen years ago, the paperback rights to *The Thorn Birds* sold for almost $2 million! Mario Puzo's *Fools Die;* Judith Krantz's best-seller *Princess Daisy;* and Scott Turow's blockbuster *Presumed Innocent* all topped that price, as did Stephen King's four-book deal with Viking Penguin (for a purported advance of $40 million). Recently, Michael Crichton, John Grisham and Patricia Cornwell hit large paydays; Cornwall recorded a three-book deal for about $24 million. The trend is up and your chances, if you're a talented writer, are better in the field of publishing than they are in gambling in Las Vegas.

When you believe you're ready to be published, you should do all you can to find a determined and dedicated agent or representative. We're out there and we need you . . . and not just because of the money. There's no bigger thrill for me than telling an author I've just found a publishing home for his book and that it will be published at long last.

Good projects sell themselves. Of course, there are many excellent writers who have written wonderful books that have yet to sell, but remember: publishing is a tricky business. One more piece of advice: I know it's a little common, but writers . . . WRITE ON!

"I always advise

writers to write

one-page synopses

of their books so

their representatives

and editors can get

a thumbnail sketch

of what the book

is about."

—*PM*

INTRODUCTION

HOW AN AGENT WORKS

Have you heard the one about the agent and the author who fly to New York from Los Angeles to meet with a publisher? The three go to lunch and when it is over, the publisher promptly pays the bill. The agent then says, "I guess we can now discuss the advance for my client." The publisher slams his hand down on the table and says, "What do you mean? I just paid it!"

My experiences as a literary agent and currently as a literary manager have involved me in the representation of many kinds of writing, including nonfiction and fiction, for book and magazine publishers. I've also worked extensively representing and packaging television series, script treatments, movies of the week, cable movies and feature films. Additionally, I've sold motion picture rights to books and magazine articles and have supervised their metamorphoses into screenplays. Currently, I'm proud to be working on many film projects. In addition, I have licensed completed films for distribution to theaters, television and/or home video. I have a breadth of experience representing the written word—not only in this country, but in foreign markets, such as England, Canada, Japan, China, Korea, Germany, Italy, Denmark, France, Holland, Spain, Portugal, Mexico and South America. I've met many aspiring authors through my public speaking work at colleges, universities, writers conferences and in private clubs. In fact, I have opted to represent many of these authors and have successfully placed books for them.

Despite my success with writers, the harsh realities of

> *the publishing business bring you to Earth quickly. So,*
> *whether you're a literary representative or a writer, get*
> *prepared for bad news! As we were going to press, Harper*
> *Collins announced it was canceling hundreds of books it*
> *had under contract.*

The publishing industry is going through enormous changes. During the past several years, there has been an overall tightening of purse strings, evident in the takeover of publishing houses and general downsizing. The book publishers' basic practice of selling books on consignment (after which large quantities of books—fifty percent on average for paperbacks—are returned from bookstores) is so antiquated that it is harming the entire industry. Despite all the successes you read about, there are many flops which go unnoticed by the public.

Because of these negative difficulties, a literary manager's belief in his client's work and the manager's assistance during the selling process cannot be underestimated. The cost of a good representative is negligible compared to the gains earned for the writer by setting up a strong and profitable business relationship with a publisher. So, let's take a positive approach to writing: *any author can improve his writing so it will be worthy of representation.*

In general, New York representatives mainly deal with book publishing and related industries, undoubtedly because New York City is the center of the book publishing world. On the other hand, Los Angeles agencies mostly deal with writers of movies and television and therefore don't spend as much time representing book authors. L.A. agents often have relationships with New York-based agencies to facilitate contact with writers who are working in publishing; conversely, New York agencies often have relationships with

Los Angeles representatives who are well-versed in the handling of movie rights for their authors. I am one of a few managers who represent all types of writing—in New York, Los Angeles and worldwide. Besides my agency in New York, which deals mostly with book authors, I have maintained a presence in Los Angeles for over twenty years, allowing me to establish myself in the motion picture, cable and television industries. In addition, my bicoastal work has afforded me the opportunity to meet all types of writers. This, in turn, has paid off in the growth of my company and in the expansion of our client base.

> *After I met Linda Evans at a party in Beverly Hills, I suggested she write a book on beauty. In a few weeks, we were talking to Simon & Schuster about it; they published it a number of years ago and it became a national best-seller. Apart from a cookbook she had already written and self-published, she was unpublished. I was able to help Linda because she needed a New York literary representative, not a Hollywood talent agent, business representative, or attorney—all of which she already had.*

The process of *networking* cannot be underestimated—it is of crucial importance to the agenting business. I meet many potential clients this way.

The art of networking is contagious. The more you do, the more likely you are to succeed. I'm where I am today because my energy level is so high that I could be walking down the street and see someone walking to the post office with a manuscript box or shipping envelope and query them . . . find out that they are carrying a novel, read it and sell it. This is true networking or just plain aggressive sales.

I met one of my most important literary clients through networking. At a party I hosted, one of my guests introduced me to William Stadiem, author of the best-selling book Marilyn Monroe Confidential. *At that time, Bill was working on a book with Vincent T. Bugliosi, the former Los Angeles District Attorney and author of* Helter Skelter. *I aggressively pursued this lead by inviting Stadiem and Bugliosi to breakfast the following morning, where I signed them as clients and represented their proposal for a nonfiction book called* The Vivian Gordon Murder Story. *The authors hadn't placed this treatment with a publisher despite their terrific track records. (Bugliosi's first book,* Helter Skelter, *about the Tate-LaBianca murders by the Charles Manson Family, sold nearly seven million copies worldwide. It was Number One on the* New York Times *Bestseller List, as were two other nonfiction books he later wrote,* And The Sea Will Tell *and* Outrage. *(Besides the books,* Marilyn Monroe Confidential *and* Too Rich, *Stadiem has authored several screenplays which were produced as movies.) Two previous representatives had tried and failed to sell their book idea and now, the ball was in my court.*

Though the proposal had been turned down by thirty-five publishers, I had faith in the property. I had them change the title to Lullaby And Good Night, *and I finally sold it to a publisher that had originally rejected it! I also sold the motion picture and television rights to ABC Entertainment. Unfortunately, it was left there, abandoned. I then re-optioned it to producers who worked with Lorimar Telepictures. They developed a first draft screenplay, which was again abandoned. I still didn't lose faith! I'm happy to say it has been optioned to another major television production company and to be made into a four-hour miniseries soon.*

One of my favorite sayings about Hollywood is: "Life is like a fishing trip—if you want to catch a big fish, you've got to go where the big fish are." When you set out to look for a literary agent, it's important that you choose one who is involved with and visible in the marketplace. Literary representatives do not simply sell an author's work and negotiate the advance. In some cases, the representative must know how to package (or, even repackage) and market the project but their primary goal is to sell it to a publisher. You may have heard that the well-respected British author Doris Lessing sent two of her manuscripts to publishers under a pseudonym. Every editor, including one at Ms. Lessing's own publishing house, rejected them. As this case details, it's not always about the writing.

> *A few years ago I represented a book on beauty called* New Beauty, *which was written by Robert L. Klein; he had tried, unsuccessfully, to get it published before he came to me.* New Beauty *was well-written, but it needed to be repackaged. I remembered briefly meeting actress Lindsay Wagner and brought Klein and Wagner together to repackage the book. Based on Wagner's involvement, it was an easier project to sell. It was published by Prentice-Hall, a division of Simon & Schuster.*

However, one does not have to be in Hollywood to sell books about famous people. For example, I represented the first *Elvis Presley Scrapbook* (an idea I came up with) for an author I was representing at the time. It was a very successful book, sold several hundred thousand copies, and was probably the first book about Presley in the marketplace that was published *before* he died.

My greatest publishing success story was when I met and took on Nancy Taylor Rosenberg as a client. Less then two months later, I had landed her a very substantial four-book, three million dollar guaranteed advance sale. (More about that later on in the chapter called Wonderful Circumstances.)

The literary representative must know the market and the people working in it. (If the literary representative's relationships in town are solid and well-grounded, then his clients have a decided edge.) The literary representative also must have confidence in his writers and in their work.

Selling a novel by my client Christopher Cook Gilmore included one of the most unusual experiences I've had as an author's rep and in defending an author's rights. I sold the synopsis and a few sample chapters of Mr. Gilmore's second novel, Watchtower, *to a publisher who had previously hired him to write a novelization. The two had a good relationship. Mr. Gilmore finished the novel, renamed* The Bad Room. *However, after the editor read it, she called to say, "Christopher Gilmore didn't write the book I hired him to write. He's going to have to do a lot of editing." Mr. Gilmore felt his novel was fine the way it was and he wasn't going to change a word for an editor who didn't appreciate the book. When I relayed this information to the editor, she said, "We don't want to publish this book. We want our money back." I offered to give the editor a postdated check in the amount of Mr. Gilmore's advance, dated sixty days away, and I would try to resell it. Actually, I had no obligation to return the advance but I was confident in the novel and that I could resell it. In two weeks, I received an offer from Avon Books for double the advance that I had previously negotiated for Mr. Gilmore and with nearly double the royalties—and he didn't have to change a word in the manuscript!*

As a writer, you must make decisions about your goals. Are you going to write category fiction, e.g., gothic, horror, western, mystery, suspense, science fiction/fantasy? Are you going to write "The Great American Novel"? Or, are you going to write for television or film? You must invest time and energy in defining the marketplace for your writing.

HOW TO GET REPRESENTATION

Almost all unknown writers need representation. Not only is it necessary for selling and negotiating contracts, it also adds to the writer's status and makes him feel like a legitimate author. However, many people have a preconceived, negative attitude toward agents and managers. As a result, those who need us sometimes approach us in an aggressive, arrogant manner. Obviously, this attitude makes it difficult for us to work for or represent them: they don't understand that if we represent them, we have a strong interest in their work! Some representatives charge a retainer, but most don't. Usually, the time your representative spends with you is his investment in your work and your future, as well as his own. Therefore, I highly recommend that you *treat your agent or representative with respect and value his time.* It will pay off for you in the long run.

You'll need to prepare an inquiry letter and a book proposal, manuscript, screenplay or teleplay, etc., when first seeking representation. Before you submit anything to a prospective representative, share it with as many people as you can. Value their feedback but weigh it carefully; don't give up your artistic integrity. Make sure your work is perfectly edited and typed. If you're writing a nonfiction book proposal, be sure it is properly developed. If the piece is a novel, particularly a first novel, it should be a completed manuscript. (It used to be possible to sell a first novel with a proposal, but this opportunity is shrinking because the market for first-time novels—known as "mid-list fiction"—

has been vanishing slowly. Since the market has changed and is continuing to change, i.e., Penguin's merger with Putnam/Berkley, publishers often have larger inventories, meaning they are less anxious to sign new deals.)

Our office receives inquiries from writers all around the world. These 200 to 500 inquiries per week (Yes, per week.) come in the form of faxes, e-mails, treatments, proposals, letters, synopses, manuscripts and screenplays. Like most representatives, we usually measure a writer's ability and originality by the quality of his inquiry letter. Therefore, we look for those well-written, perfectly edited, typed and presented letters or proposals or better yet, manuscripts.

I always advise an author to write a one-page synopsis of his property so publishers and editors can get a thumbnail sketch of what the book is about. In addition, when I've got a meeting with a potential publisher, it's easier for me to take a one-page synopsis than it is to carry a bulky manuscript. (If I ever write my autobiography, I think I'll call it *Born to Schlep*!) If the editor likes the idea, I then follow up by sending the complete manuscript; this way, I save myself stress AND lower-back problems. A few years ago, I began asking our authors to add to the package a paragraph or two about themselves. I have successfully sold this book-and-author package a number of times.

If you need to know more about particular agencies (i.e., what type of writing they represent, what genres they most often sell, etc.), send a *query* (or, information) *letter* requesting such information, or take a look at *Literary Market Place* (LMP) or the annual *Writer's Market;* both of these reference guides include basic agency information. *Jeff Herman's Agency Guide* is also a good resource. We are building a web site for my company that will be an invaluable resource to authors.

I opened this Introduction with one of William Saroyan's famous quotes. The valuable message in these valuable words, from my perspective as a businessman and literary representative, is that we're a reflection of the quality of the material we represent.

> *"I made a fiasco out of my life, but look at the material I had to work with."*
> —William Saroyan

[Note: When I was a member of the Saroyan Theatre Dept. At Mammoth College, the first play I auditioned for was Saroyan's The Time of Your Life. *Luckily, I got the lead role of "Nick," the bartender. I studied Saroyan; and his quote (above) is most apropos in my line of work.]*

"The representative

is ultimately the

employee of the

author, though,

and the author

should know how

and when it is

appropriate

to use them."

—*PM*

CHAPTER ONE

PROTOCOL

A critic is a man who knows the way but can't drive the car.
—Kenneth Tynan

MANUSCRIPT PROTOCOL

Every writer interested in having his book published or his screenplay produced should follow correct protocol when presenting his query letter to a potential buyer. Not only does this fall under the rubric of good etiquette, but it also goes a long way toward convincing potential buyers that you are a professional who is aware of and observes professional norms. In this sense, writing is no different from any other business: small details matter in a large way. Your proposal or manuscript is only a tool to help you make the sale . . . but the better-looking the tool, the better chance you have of success.

Perhaps the most common violation of protocol that crosses my desk is the submission of a handwritten manuscript. It's safe to say that when one of these is received, the writing is usually illegible. But even if you have the finest handwriting in the world, it is still an unacceptable submission, especially given the widespread availability and affordability of home computers and the reasonable cost of typing services. As a result, the readers for my company are instructed never to read handwritten manuscripts; they should, instead, move on to a submission by a writer who cares enough about his work to take the time to present it in a clean, legible format.

Similarly, all correspondence accompanying a submission should be typewritten; your prospective representative or publisher should not have to decipher what you've written and miscommunication between the two of you will be kept to a minimum. I also strongly believe in letters—not faxes or e-mails—especially for the first communiqué with a prospective representative. (I was shocked—and not happy—when an unsolicited author e-mailed his complete manuscript to me!)

Another violation of protocol is the submission of a sloppy manuscript. This could be defined as:

- A manuscript in poor condition, i.e., dog-eared or dirty pages, sloppily typed, etc.;
- A manuscript printed on a low-quality dot-matrix printer, making a photocopy of it especially difficult to read;
- A manuscript that is improperly bound.

The *proper manuscript* is, in fact, one that *is unbound* (the pages are left loose for easy handling by the reader), typed on 8.5" x 11" bond or semi-bond paper (one side only) and mailed in a strong cardboard box. Binders or folders are NOT recommended: they make the manuscript too awkward to handle when reading.

Equally crucial is *correct pagination*. The main purpose of paginating an unpublished manuscript is to facilitate finding a particular page in a hurry.

I received a manuscript from a published writer—which means he should have known better—that was not only typed with a bad, overly-used ribbon, but was unpaginated. We were under a deadline to get this manu-

script to a publisher when we discovered that it had been incorrectly photocopied. As a result, we had to re-collate the manuscript and we very nearly missed the deadline. The unpaginated manuscript was a mistake that might have caused serious professional embarrassment to the writer and to us.

Proper pagination for a manuscript begins on the first page of the book—not on the Title page, the Table of Contents page, the Acknowledgment page or the Dedication page—and it proceeds to the end of the manuscript without pause. Pagination is not broken down by chapters; all illustration pages are included. In addition, simple pagination (numerals printed in the upper right-hand corner) is best. The dogmatic insistence upon pagination may seem irrelevant to the quality of the writing, but a small matter such as this can affect a reader's judgment of the overall work, which could tip the balance when decisions are made.

RELATIONSHIP PROTOCOL

There is also a protocol for writers to follow when interacting with representatives and publishers. First of all, any relationship with a representative or publisher should be treated as a business relationship. For example, when I agree to *consider* a proposal or manuscript for representation, it is not tantamount to my agreement to *represent* it. Authors who understand this will allow a reasonable amount of time for me to evaluate their work and to come to my own conclusions about its viability. Pressure from a writer trying to "sell" me usually has an adverse effect: it is more than likely to turn me off from his project altogether. I consider myself the "hunter," not the "hunted." Novice writers must understand that most reputable agencies handle an enormous amount of submissions and, quite frankly, because they are unpublished, they are placed at the bottom of the reading pile. (Your hard work and determination—and patience—can change that. So, when you do secure representation for your writing, it still does not exempt you from the editorial protocol laid out in this chapter.)

Agents and managers, like editors and publishers, are extremely busy people. It is not that we're unfriendly or that we don't want to know about your new project; it's just that we need to restrict communication to matters of real importance. Too many worthless phone calls and too much correspondence requiring responses harms your representative's ability to work productively for you and for the other authors he represents. Some writers expect their representatives to be hand-holders or psychiatrists or publicity flaks or lawyers or bankers or friends. Principally, representatives negotiate the best possible sale for an author's work—this is what we're paid to do and it is enough. But, as a company, we have done much more than just sell a client's work. We have gotten many of our clients national publicity, offered poignant editorial advice and even given authors ideas for books.

However, the representative works for the author; as your "employee," you should know how and when you can turn to him for help. The representative should answer any questions you have about contractual details concerning your book. Unfortunately, a writer often becomes so engrossed in his work as his publishing deadline approaches that he cannot resist talking directly to his editor. The result?

- The writer dictates to his publishing house how to publish his book (into which the house has likely already made a substantial investment);
- An editor whose excitement for the project is dampened by constant author harassment; and
- A writer who has far fewer answers than he was hoping for.

Many basic queries from a first-time author can be answered without difficulty by an experienced representative. Those questions which he cannot answer will likely require the additional weight of his reputation when brought up with a publisher. (This is when the agent begins the conversation by saying, "In all my years as an agent . . . .")

Frequently, the writer and his rep can play the good cop/bad cop scenario with the publisher: the author is responsible for the terrific writing and the devotion to his project, while the complaints about the contract, advance, royalties, tardiness in editorial response, expenses, etc., come from the representative. This scenario is editorial protocol at its finest—everyone knows his job and treats each other with respect: the writer is successfully published, the representative secures a potentially lucrative new client and the publisher gets a great book.

The deal is made.

"A nonfiction book proposal should simply answer all the questions that an editor who might be considering the book would be inclined to ask."

—PM

CHAPTER TWO

NONFICTION

*The telephone book is full of facts,
but it doesn't contain a single idea.*
　　　　　　　　—Mortimer J. Adler

THE DEVELOPMENT AND CREATION
OF A NONFICTION BOOK PROPOSAL

A nonfiction work is defined as writing derived from fact; or, for the most part, it is a piece that is fact-based. From a literary representative's point of view, selling a nonfiction book is easier than selling a novel. Works of nonfiction include the following genres:
- biography (authorized, "as-told-to" or unauthorized);
- crime (true or anthology);
- how-to (on any subject);
- history (including performing arts and entertainment histories);
- war;
- science (including anthropology and medical);
- travel;
- cookbook; and
- any fact-based account on any subject.

Virtually all nonfiction books my company has represented (roughly half the books we have represented in total) have sold from a proposal.

An editor told me that a nonfiction book proposal should anticipate and then answer all questions that any editor might be inclined to ask. Aside from the book's topic and other related details, these questions might include the following:

- How long will the book be (in pages and in word length)?
- Will the book be illustrated (with what kind of illustrations)?
- How long it will it take to write?
- And (most importantly), why will this book be better than any other book on its subject that has ever been published?

My company once considered representing a book on female infertility. The book was eloquently written and the author was knowledgeable on the subject. However, after looking at Books in Print, *we discovered there already were dozens of books published on the topic. We decided not to represent a book in what was already an overcrowded marketplace.*

While I was trying to place this book—the one in your hands that you are now reading—I learned that numerous books on writing are readily available. However, I also discovered that:

- no book was written specifically from the agent's or manager's point of view; and
- few addressed the topic of what an author can do to make his work more sellable.

I, thus, patterned this book for the available market and was sure to include samples of book proposals for the potential author to study (found in the Appendices).

I recently sold a book called *Open Boundaries* written by Howard Sherman and Ron Schultz, to Addison Wesley for $75,000.[1] The author incorporated tips from Richard Carlson's philosophy on selling (Mr. Carlson is the president of the Carlson National Group, a national communication and sales consulting company) into his own proposal, to help him sell his idea. Carlson's philosophy presents the following theories:

- The decision to publish a book is based on *The Verified Need,* which is the discovery of too few or too many books on the same topic. This Need is based on factual information, not hearsay or guestimation.
- *The Felt Need,* which is based on opinion, asks, "Why is the Verified Need intolerable or unacceptable?" This opinion should not belong solely to the author, but it also should represent the opinion of experts. Once the Verified Need has been established, the Felt Need follows.
- According to Carlson, the Felt Need is followed by the *Verifiable Benefit,* which asks, "What will the reader gain from this book that can't be found elsewhere?" Like the Verified Need, the response to this question is based on fact and evidence, not on the hopes and wishes of the author.
- Finally, the author should provide the *Felt Benefit,* or, how long the book will succeed. The Felt Benefit is based on the author's opinion.

As Carlson clearly states, "When all four of these issues are addressed in this particular order, there is a reason to buy and an opportunity to sell."

Schultz makes sure that these four points are incorporated and addressed within the first three to four parts of his book proposal, yet he does not individually highlight them so the reader is almost unaware of this successful sales technique.

---

1. *Open Boundaries* will be published by Addison Wesley for their Spring/Summer 1998 list.

Listed below is a brief description of what my company has used as a guideline for developing a nonfiction book proposal. Of course, different kinds of nonfiction book proposals will vary, but most often, they incorporate the same basic points.

STRUCTURING A NONFICTION PROPOSAL

Before a publisher can make an offer to a writer, he must know some basic, pertinent facts about the book. These facts should be included in every proposal:

- the approximate number of pages;
- the total number of words (75,000 to 125,000 words is an average length);
- the type of format;
- the number and type of illustrations and how the illustrations will be presented (i.e., color, black-and-white, graphs, charts, etc.).

The publisher needs this information in order to calculate the correct advance payment against the writer's anticipated earnings during the book's first year of publication.

Following is the standard format our writers use when presenting a nonfiction book:

1. A *Book/Author Sheet* that would read like the copy on the book jacket; it should include several paragraphs about the book and one paragraph about the author.

2. An *Introduction, Preface,* and/or *Foreword* to the book.

3. A few paragraphs from the author addressing the question, *"Why should you publish this book?"* The author should discuss the book's available market and how his book would differ from others on the same topic.

4. A *Table of Contents,* briefly listing the chapters and including a few sentences about each chapter.

5. A few *sample chapters*, normally the *first three*, unless there is a cogent reason to provide later chapters. The samples should illustrate the author's writing ability and show that it is professional and delivers publishable, acceptable prose.
6. If the book includes illustrations or photographs,
   samples of these also should be included.

This material should be assembled in a neat, professional
manner. All pages should be typed, double-spaced, on bond
paper; wide margins should be used. If the book is typed on
a computer, only a letter-quality or laser printer is acceptable. All photocopies should be of the highest quality.

ABOUT APPENDIX A . . .

Appendix A includes several samples of Nonfiction Book
Proposals; these have been used successfully to market works
by authors my company represents.

The first is Lee Butcher's *The Accidental Millionaire: The
Rise and Fall of Steve Jobs at Apple Computer* (see Appendix A,
No. 1), an unauthorized biography of Jobs, the creator and
former chief executive of Apple Computers. Butcher was
formerly the editor of the *San Jose Business Journal*, which
covers events in Silicon Valley, so he was in a unique position to write this book: he witnessed the rift between Steve
Jobs and Apple's new executive John Sculley and had plenty
of inside information on the power struggle. As an established writer, Butcher created a successful proposal by opening with a complete overview of the story; he then offered a
detailed, chapter-by-chapter breakdown of the book. The
proposal concluded with his argument on how the book
would fit into the current literary marketplace. He also included a brief statement about his work as an editor and
about his ability to write the biography. The book was first
published by Paragon House; its trade paperback edition
was published a year later. Finally, the mass-market paper-

back rights were sold to Knightsbridge Publishing. The motion picture and television rights were optioned to Chessman/Main Films and the project currently is in development as a feature film. If you study Butcher's proposal carefully and if you have the right subject—someone timely and well-known—you, too, could duplicate the success of *The Accidental Millionaire.*

True crime is another genre of publishing that has become very active over the past several years. Since every major crime is first covered in the newspapers, there often is interest from readers who would like more detailed information, so the crime then is written up as a book. Many times, the book is optioned for a Movie of the Week or miniseries. I was approached by a writer named Steven Salerno, whose first true crime, *Deadly Blessing,* was successfully published in hardcover by William Morrow and in paperback by St. Martin's Press. He approached me with an idea for a new book, tentatively entitled *Fatal Freeway,* about the murder of a college student named Cara Knott by Craig Allan Peyer, a thirty-six-year-old California Highway Patrol Officer, outside San Diego. Salerno developed a seventeen-page proposal (see Appendix A, No. 2). I sent his proposal to twenty publishers interested in true crime. Of these, more than a half-dozen wanted to buy it. We auctioned the book to Clarkson N. Potter; it was scheduled for hardcover publication, in Spring, 1991. Furthermore, the television and motion picture rights were optioned to a major Los Angeles-based television production company. Unfortunately, the book was never published or produced.

Marketing this particular book on true crime was problematic for several reasons:

- At the time Salerno and I began soliciting the sale of the book, the case for Cara Knott's murderer had not yet gone to trial.

- When the case eventually did go to trial, with Peyer as the defendant, no verdict was delivered due to a hung jury. (Peyer was retried later that year and was convicted of first-degree murder; he is now serving his sentence.)
- Because Peyer never testified at his own trials, Salerno was faced with the difficult task of writing the book without testimony from the convicted murderer.

The structure of any story is the first element to be considered by editors, potential producers and network executives when they examine new projects. Therefore, a good rule of thumb for gauging the potential success of a true crime nonfiction book, motion picture or television project is whether or not the crime has a clear beginning, middle and end—the standards of drama that make any story accessible.

An excellent illustration of this rule comes from Ernest Hemingway. More than twenty years ago, at the beginning of my career, I had lunch with a well-established newspaper syndicator who told me the following story: Ernest Hemingway was lunching at Luchow's with several writers, claiming he could write a six-word-long short story. The other writers balked. Hemingway told them to ante up ten dollars apiece. If he was wrong, he would match it; if he was right, he would keep the pot. He quickly wrote six words on a napkin and passed it around. The words were: "For Sale, Baby Shoes, Never Worn." Papa won the bet: his short story was complete. It had a beginning, a middle and an end!

However, like all rules, there is an occasional exception. For example, when Claus von Bulow was arrested for the attempted murder of his wife Sunny, the jury also could not reach a verdict, but, nevertheless, the story was released as a feature film starring Jeremy Irons as Claus and Glenn Close as Sunny (*Reversal Of Fortune*—Warner Bros., 1990; Barbet Schroeder, 112 mins.). This scenario did not work for *Fatal Freeway* because a book or movie deal might have been jeopardized if Peyer had not been convicted. For the Knott family, Peyer's late conviction provided the closure they needed.

My company has enjoyed a wonderful relationship with well-known author Ted Sennett, who has written over a dozen books on the performing arts, including *Warner Bros. Presents, Great Hollywood Movies, Hollywood Musicals, The Art of Hanna-Barbera*. When Sennett first decided to write *Hollywood's Golden Year: 1939* (see Appendix A, No. 3), he created a proposal similar to those he had created for all his books. This proposal was vital in placing *Hollywood's Golden Year: 1939* with St. Martin's Press. Sennett's idea for this book was very specific: the year, 1939, was one of the most celebrated in film history and he wanted the opportunity to write lovingly about some of his favorite movies. Because Sennett already was an established author on performing arts, it wasn't necessary for him to write a lengthy proposal (his extensive credits spoke for themselves). His brief five-page proposal was thorough and impressive and played an integral part in the marketing of the book. After its publication, it received marvelous reviews and was sold to several book clubs.

Roy Guste's *New Orleans Creole Cookery: The Definitive Work on its History and Development* is another example of a nonfiction book sold on the basis of its proposal (see Appendix A, No. 4). The story of this book's sale should encourage you to believe in your work and to find an aggressive representative who believes in you, too. And, it should help you understand that, ultimately, it takes only one publisher/editor for your book to find a home.

Chef Roy F. Guste, Jr., sent a copy of one of his previously published cookbooks to me, along with an invitation to join him for a meal at his family-owned restaurant in New Orleans, called Antoine's. I had been invited to speak at the New Orleans Writers Conference, so Roy and I arranged to meet. Little did I know that Roy was anxious to meet every representative attending the conference, six in all, and every editor or publisher attending; he had probably contacted them all! During our meal, Roy told me about his book, a complete and fascinating history of Creole cooking. He went on to say how fortunate any rep would be to have him as a client. He assured me that he had a wealth of literary properties and that cookbooks were not his only area of expertise. He explained that every representative attending the conference wanted to represent him. He didn't particularly like reps and so I should tell him what could I do for him that the others couldn't. I had already fallen in love with the project and Roy's personal explanation of it left a lasting impression. (So lasting, in fact, that I used much of his sales pitch to me when I later went to sell it to publishers!) After much discussion and, after getting to know Roy better, he asked that my company and I represent him. The first publisher I contacted found the project exciting and agreed to publish it, but only if contained lavish illustrations (at least 100 color photographs and 200 black-and-white illustrations). The publishing house also disclosed that, despite their enthusiasm, they couldn't make us a firm offer for at least six weeks. I used those weeks to explore other possibilities, but I found that other publishers were more wary of the property; most felt the market was glutted with books on this topic. Furthermore, the cookbook industry is noted for having either big winners or big losers; some editors didn't think Roy's book was a safe enough bet. Viking Studio Books—the original house that was interested—invited Roy to New York to make a presentation. It was one of the best I ever have seen! Roy's belief in his work, combined with his vast knowledge of the subject and juxtaposed against his charismatic style (à la Tom Wolfe, bow tie included) completely won them over.

Years ago, I met a talented speech writer named Joan Detz, who wanted to write a how-to book on speech-making. She wrote a brief proposal for a book called *How to Write and Give Great Speeches! A Practical Guide for Executives*. Her proposal did not meet my usual requirements for nonfiction proposals (and, it was only three pages long!). But, we sold the book to the first (and only) publisher that saw it, St. Martin's Press. To Detz's credit, her proposal (short as it was) was well-written and illustrated her professionalism. In addition, she was able to find a niche in an area of publishing (the self-help or how-to genre), of which the public never seems to tire. *How To Write and Give Great Speeches!* was first published in 1984, and has been updated and reprinted several times. Detz's brief proposal (see Appendix A, No. 5) may help you decide if your area of expertise is appropriate for a book in this nonfiction genre.

The final example of a successful nonfiction proposal (see Appendix A, No. 6) is Dr. Albert Marchetti's proposal for *Beating the Odds*. After reading Marchetti's first proposal, I sent it back to him with some suggestions for improvement. Because of its topic and the potential for complex language, the proposal included a detailed definition of the book idea, plus a description of all components, including:

- A description of the book;
- Why this book was necessary;
- The book's intended audience;
- The book's chief competition;
- The style and tone of the book;
- The author's credentials;
- The author's marketability;
- A Table of Contents page;

- A paragraph describing each of the chapters in the book.
- "A Closing Word."

After he revised the proposal, we submitted it to several publishers, successfully placing the book with Contemporary Books, Inc. And then it was published in paperback by St. Martin's Press.

The importance of a highly professional, accurate and well-conceived proposal may be the difference between getting published and not. Good luck with your proposal(s)!

"All novelists

should think

about structure in

their careers."

—*PM*

CHAPTER THREE

FICTION

Writing is turning one's worst moments into money.
—J.P. Donleavy

This chapter is devoted to some of the interactions I have had with novelists, as well as to experiences I've had developing and placing novels with publishers around the world. During twenty-five years as a literary representative, my respect for novelists has grown tremendously. Don't misunderstand: writing a nonfiction book is an incredible accomplishment. However, all nonfiction, no matter how difficult or time-consuming the research and writing can be, is based on facts; they rule the work. On the other hand, novels are complete creations, borne of the writer's thoughts and emotions. According to my observation of effective novels I have read and represented, the formula for successful fiction is:

1. Have a great story to tell—one with a beginning, a middle and an end.
2. Make sure your novel is well-structured.
3. Tell your story stylistically and as well as you possibly can.
4. Make sure the elements of your novel are well-developed: the plotting is solid, the conflict is convincing and the characters are well-defined.

As you all know, writing is a lonely business. So, before you sit down to create a 300-page manuscript (at 300 words per page), be sure that your idea is original or exciting enough to be worthy of your time, energy and emotions.

While standard novels are between 300 and 500 manuscript pages, there are exceptions to this rule: Jonathan Livingston Seagull *and* The Bridges of Madison County *both were highly successful short novels.*

It is quite a challenge creating a manuscript, complete with beginning, middle and end, not to mention infusing the work with lively and original characters and a solid and clever plot while presenting it in a style that keeps the reader riveted to the page!

TRENDS

The climate for fiction has changed since the 1970s, when I first became a literary representative. In those days, it was possible to sell a novel from a strong proposal (i.e., a brief outline and several sample chapters). If the subject of the novel was based on a topical news event, publishers often were inclined to move quickly and take a risk. Today's marketplace is different: publishers are less willing to gamble. Consequently, in order to sell a novel today, it is imperative that the author submits a *completed, polished draft.* (Occasionally, I will look at the first 100 pages of a novel; if I find it absolutely spellbinding and have complete belief in the author to finish his work, I MAY recommend it to a few editors. But, this is rare.)

People I meet often want to know what kind of trends I foresee in publishing. Trends are always changing, which makes my responses change, too. For example, if someone had talked to me several years ago about writing an espionage novel about Libya or one that contained villainous Soviets, I would have encouraged him. Now, however, Russia-bashing is definitely "out" and books about Libya have over saturated the market. (In fact, forget about the Middle East altogether.) Do keep in mind that new and interesting product is always welcome in the categories of suspense or male adventure.

When thinking of fresh and different concepts, you should juxtapose the word "different" against the traditions of publishing. For example, pornography was popular in the 1970s, but now it is passé. Also in the '70s, gothic romances were in vogue but now they are out of fashion. One way to develop a new idea for a novel is to frequent bookstores and ask the proprietor or his employees what the upcoming trends look like to them. Also, consult authors, editors, representatives—whoever is available to you in the industry.

Whenever a client asks me or an associate about developing a particular story idea, we hope he takes our advice seriously. If he doesn't believe us, we want him to tell us why so we can press our point. Or, perhaps he will pursue the development of his idea elsewhere and return to us. To me, it's a representative's fiduciary obligation to discuss an author's idea in the context of the current demands of the literary marketplace. (For example, if an author with an established reputation for historical love stories decides to write a slasher novel, it's going to be difficult for the representative to place that work—the author is trying a whole new genre in which he is an unknown quantity.)

When preparing to write your own novel, read as much as you can. Study the styles of your favorite authors. Try to notice the trends that are important to you. And consider the fact that it is possible to emulate a successful author's work. For example, Tom Clancy's novel, *The Hunt For Red October*, was the start of the "techno-thriller." It not only was a wildly successful book but it also became a block-buster movie. The key to this book's success was Clancy's ability to research the subject so thoroughly that the results leapt from the headlines and onto the page; there wasn't an element in *Hunt* that didn't ring true. If you study Clancy's work, you may be able to craft your own techno-thriller. Take a look at Stephen King: he is a contemporary (or, "re-incarnation" might be a better description) of Edgar Allan Poe, having become the modern-day master of the maca-bre. Although it would be preferable to create your own niche and not be compared to another writer, it's not a bad thing being compared to a successful writer (i.e., this new author's novel has "the pace of a Tom Clancy techno-thriller" or "the richness of a James A. Michener historical saga" or "the suspense and horrific originality of Stephen King").

All novelists should think about structuring their ca-reers. If one of my authors decides to break into publishing by writing westerns, I hope that after he writes a few books in this category, he'll graduate into writing a western saga or a family saga or, perhaps, developing his own series. It would be unfortunate for an author to develop a track record as a western novelist, only to proceed to the horror genre. Pub-lishers like to know that when they invest their time and money launching an author's career, it will be a profitable exercise for them as they capitalize on the growth and suc-cess of that author.

CATEGORY FICTION

One reason that selling fiction today is difficult is because of the disappearance of what was once known as Midlist Fiction. Midlist Fiction was an area of publishing that in-corporated category fiction as well as a possible starting ground for new authors. The economics have changed. Pub-lishers are interested only in the bottom line.

There is another area of fiction that used to be viable for novice writers. Paperback publishers consistently publish *Category Fiction*, which is known as a staple of the industry. These are books in genres such as, western, mystery, horror, science fiction and fantasy. For example, New American Library developed a "Trailsman Adult Western" series, which has published 200+ books. Each book usually sells between 50,000 and 70,000 copies; they are published in several foreign languages. You can see now that writing for a series can keep any author busy. However, breaking into Category Fiction is difficult now and the advances paid to the authors—particularly those who work under pseudonyms or who write for series that are owned by a publisher—are small (often as low as $3,000 to $6,000), as are the royalties. My best advice on this score is to believe in your talent and to create your own original work.

SERIES FICTION

An area of publishing that has become popular in the original paperback field is *Series Fiction*. Over the years I've developed several new series—novels initially intended as single works but, due to their popularity, become long-term series. (One was Sarah Lovett's "Sylvia Strange" series with Villard/Fawcett, a division of Random House.) If I have clients whose books have open endings and continuing characters, I usually encourage them to consider creating Series Fiction and, I believe, I advise them correctly.

One of my clients had an idea to write a piece on The Jersey Devil, a legendary folk character from the Garden State. He sold a fantasy essay to Atlantic City Magazine *based on this character (see Appendix B). Although I always counsel my clients to submit completed fiction, the editor found this work combined the writing styles of Anne*

Rice, Richard Condon and Nathaniel West and that it was a fresh approach to an old folk legend. His article launched a three-book series which was sold for publication (it was never completed due to the bankruptcy of the publisher).

U.S. publishers turn out so many books a year, an author must think carefully about the series he plans to develop. For example, I would not advise creating a new western series now, but a Male Adventure series set in an exotic, unexplored part of the world would be a viable choice.

Ten major paperback publishers and approximately twenty imprint publishers produce between ten and twenty titles per month, or 300 original paperback books, per publishing company per year.

LITERARY FICTION

Should you opt to write a serious (literary) novel, be sure you are properly prepared. Today, it is not enough to write a beautiful, literary masterpiece; you also must develop the patience to ride the bumpy obstacle course necessary to get it published.

We currently represent a wonderful first novel that, so far, has been turned down by more than twenty publishers. Ironically, the rejection letters glow with superlatives for the author. These types of rejections are good for the ego but not for the pocketbook, so buck up and don't get too discouraged by rejection.

Choose your ideas carefully and keep abreast of them. Read consistently about a subject that interests you. For example, if you like political thrillers, read about the political and military activity that threatens to take place in Mexico, Central America, South America and possibly Korea over the next several years. These countries could provide a hotbed of material for Male and/or Female Adventure fiction.

If the genre you opt to write for is in original paperbacks, your books will not be reviewed by the consumer press who use the little space they devote to books to review hard covers. Consequently, you must carefully weigh the option of breaking into publishing via writing for Category or Series Fiction or by taking the longer (perhaps more difficult) road of creating a name for yourself with a more "serious" work of fiction. A first hardcover novel with a small initial print run that sells only 6,000 to 10,000 copies—if widely and favorably reviewed—will launch an author's career more dramatically than an original paperback book that sells three times that amount.

CRITICISM

Everyone who creates—whether it is a novel, nonfiction book, movie, piece of art—must deal with *criticism,* which is defined as "the art of evaluating or analyzing works of art or literature."[2] This sounds easy enough to accept, but for most creators, accepting criticism is as difficult as the act of creating itself.

2. *Webster's Ninth New Collegiate Dictionary.* Springfield, MA: Merriam-Webster Inc., 1991.

Essay

TWO THUMBS DOWN:
Dealing with Criticism

by Jennifer Robinson[3]

At a recent writer's conference, a client was asked when she felt her novels were completely finished. "When I'm signing copies in a bookstore," she replied. "I like to change things constantly." A writer who is not just willing but *eager* to rewrite (and rewrite and rewrite) is worth his or her weight in gold.

During the years I've worked with Peter Miller—on virtually all the fiction we've represented—I've never seen a book leave our office without having been reworked extensively.

While fiction may seem intimate and personal—a total, individual expression of *who you are*—it doesn't mean the piece won't need the fresh eye of an astute reader in order to flower fully. Indeed, it's probably *because* fiction is so personal that it needs constructive criticism—the writer is too close to it and is unable (or unwilling) to see its flaws. Your novel is your baby: quite literally, you gave birth to it. And so, to you, it may seem like a beautiful, flawless jewel. But, in most cases, it's not. The sooner you realize this, the sooner you will admit that someone else might see its flaws. Then, the faster you'll correct them and the closer you'll be to having your work published. Taking pride in your work is vital; seeing every word as sacrosanct is deadly.

---

3. Jennifer Robinson is Vice President and Head of Development at PMA and has been working with me for almost ten years. She's one of the best editors I've worked with and has helped champion our cause of keeping hard cover fiction alive.

Everyone is going to make comments on your novel; your agent will be the first in a line of many. As representatives, we find it necessary to do some editing—sometimes minor, sometimes extensive—on every novel we represent. Selling new fiction is difficult in any case, but if the work is imperfect ("close but not quite"), it's nearly impossible. When we submit a novel to editors, we must feel confident the book is in the best shape possible, then the editor will come into the picture. Editors have their own opinion on a piece, their own ideas of how a novel can improve. However, after you are published, the criticism doesn't stop. If you're lucky, you'll get lots of reviews; if you're not so lucky, those reviews will be bad. If you have no patience for your agent's criticism (remember, he's the one who loves your book and wants it to succeed), then the cold, cruel world of publishing (and snarky reviewers who *love* to flex their muscles by wittily trashing others' efforts) will be intolerable.

The clients we work with best, those who navigate the shoals of publishing most expertly, are the ones who listen to criticism and, in fact, relish it. They're the writers who are excited by new ideas, new directions, new possibilities for their work; they're the ones who know that any good idea or interesting alteration will only make their piece better and that having the best book possible is, after all, the whole point. Writers who revile criticism, who won't listen to it or who shy away from writing after they receive it, run into stumbling blocks throughout their careers. They certainly will have difficulty getting an agent, getting published, finding an audience.

Criticism can be a writer's best friend.

As a writer, you must:

- Learn to *accept* criticism;
- Be able to *learn* from criticism;
- Get to *love* criticism.

Otherwise, your work (and your career) will never be as successful as it can be.

In an attempt to present unpublished writers with the idea of accepting criticism—and to loosen them up a bit—I created the following questionnaire for a writer's workshop on criticism I attended. This obviously is a lighthearted attempt at teaching novice writers how to deal with criticism, but the underlying message is serious.

So, take the test and see what your Criticism IQ is.

WHAT IS YOUR CRITICISM IQ?

1. When I finish a draft of my work I...
   a) FedEx it to Judith Regan.
   b) put it in my sock drawer.
   c) give it to a trusted friend to read.
   d) have a Martini.

2. I have considered joining a writers' group because I'm...
   a) lonely.
   b) interested in the expressive flow of ideas and criticism in a nonthreatening atmosphere where I might learn something and improve my craft.
   c) addicted to the free donuts.
   d) anxious to read the work of writers who are worse than I am.

3. Maxwell Perkins is...
   a) that guy on *Mutual of Omaha's Wild Kingdom.*
   b) the inventor of instant coffee.
   c) the chauffeur on *Hart to Hart.*
   d) legendary editor of Hemingway, Fitzgerald and Wolfe.

4. When someone tells me he doesn't like my work I...
   a) kick him where it hurts.
   b) go off to a corner and cry.
   c) thoughtfully consider what he's saying and why.
   d) fill out my application for air-conditioning repairman school.

5. I consider the optimum number of drafts on any work to be...
   a) One.
   b) Two.
   c) Thirty-two.
   d) however many it takes.

6. People who criticize my work are...
   a) unhappy, unfulfilled wannabe writers who hate me.
   b) messengers of Satan.
   c) trying to help my career.
   d) sorry as soon as I get hold of them.

7. If some who critiques my book gives me a new idea that I use, I will...
   a) be revealed as a shameless fraud on *Oprah.*
   b) become impotent.
   c) never write anything good ever again.
   d) still get my name on the book cover.

8. I believe that every word I write is...
   a) golden.
   b) English.
   c) really quite bad, but don't tell anyone.
   d) a work-in-progress.

9. An editor's central function is to...
   a) give me vast sums of money.
   b) become my best friend.
   c) offer extensive and detailed criticism of my work so it will be as good as it can be.
   d) yell, "Stop the presses!"

10. An agent who offers editorial advice is...
    a) cruisin' for a bruisin'.
    b) suffering from delusions of grandeur.
    c) wasting time when he should be on the phone making me a deal.
    d) trying to make my book more marketable.

11. I won't change my work unless...
    a) I'm paid an enormous advance.
    b) someone offers me some clever advice.
    c) Michelle Pfeiffer/Andy Garcia gives me a foot massage.
    d) hell freezes over.

12. I will only take advice from...
    a) Sonny Mehta.
    b) my mechanic about my car, but only if I'm sure he's not trying to fleece me.
    c) anyone with something valid to say.
    d) Dionne Warwick.

13. The best criticism is...
   a) no criticism.
   b) in the *New York Times.*
   c) honest, respectful and constructive.
   d) offered by me.

14. The most important thing about writing is...
   a) having a good computer with all the latest software.
   b) being a lawyer from Mississippi.
   c) having a first cousin who works at Simon & Schuster.
   d) rewriting.

Now, let someone you trust read your novel and give you his comments; he should be thorough; he could be merciless. Listen to his criticism and take it with strength. Then go and criticize someone else's work: at least it will make you feel better!

"When a publisher really wants an author, or a particular book, they are willing to make changes on the contract to which they would normally not agree."

—PM

CHAPTER FOUR

WONDERFUL CIRCUMSTANCES

*"Most writers can write books faster
than publishers can write checks."*
—*Richard Curtis*

On the first Saturday of January 1992 I went to the post office, collected the mail and went to work where I began sorting through the barrage of correspondence and submissions.

In 1992, my agency was receiving between twenty-five and 100 new submissions each week. Currently, we log between 200 and 500 per week.

One of the submissions I opened that day was headed for the "slush pile." It was an unsolicited submission from an unknown author named Nancy Taylor Rosenberg, consisting of a substantial portion of her first novel, *Mitigating Circumstances.* It was logged and given to a new reader in the company, Catherine Garnier, who began reading it and was immediately impressed. Having previously worked for a major film producer, Catherine was struck by the compelling story and also by the work's obvious film potential. On the basis of her evaluation, I read the first chapters and was dazzled. I forwarded the manuscript to our senior reader and Director of Development, Jennifer Robinson. I wanted Jennifer to read the entire manuscript and give me her comments; as one of my senior associates, I trust her judgment implicitly. Next, I arranged to meet Rosenberg in San Diego, California, the following week. (I like to meet potential clients in person.) I already had planned to be in San Diego to speak at the Southern California Writer's Conference and Nancy's home was in nearby Laguna Niguel.

When we met, Nancy handed me the latest draft of her manuscript and asked if my agency would give her advice on rewriting and polishing it. I agreed to have this done for her. From the first moments of our meeting, I was struck by Nancy's candor and her drive. I also was intrigued by her former association with the Dallas Police Department and by the fact that she is a native Texan.

My affinity for Texans dates back to 1987, when I gave my first speech at the University of Texas at Dallas. I have had a lot of positive activity with Texas authors: my agency has successfully represented over sixty books by Texans in the last decade! And, most importantly, my wonderful wife Giselle hails from Fort Worth.

On the plane back to New York, I read about fifty pages of her revised manuscript and I was riveted. Nancy's storytelling style draws the reader in as the plot unfolds; she adds layer upon layer of suspense and intrigue. It is a wonderful experience to read a novel that only gets better and more suspenseful as it progresses.

Two weeks later, although our report on her manuscript was not quite finished, I called her. She asked me directly: "Do you want to represent me?" I responded, "Yes!" Nancy then mentioned that several other agents had offered to represent her and were inundating her with calls. I told her how effective our agency would be for her, particularly when books have motion picture potential. I promised to send her our notes the next day, to be followed up by a contract. Nancy was impressed by our six-page report; she wanted to sign with us and asked me how to handle the other agents. I told her to be as honest and direct with them as she was with me.

> *When an agent is ready to sign an author, it's like a man proposing marriage to a woman: the agent offers the writer a "ring" because he wants to "marry" the author; the author, then, should do the right thing: show the other "boyfriends" the engagement ring and tell them to quit knocking on the door.*

Nancy is an indefatigable writer, capable of working twelve hours a day, nonstop. She is, quite simply, the stuff literary representatives and publishers dream of. Based on our notes, she quickly completed a revised version of her book. Jennifer spent an entire day reading the manuscript one more time. We faxed Nancy our notes; she promised to tend to the last polish immediately.

Nancy was about seventy-five percent completed with the manuscript when I began calling publishers. I knew that many were seeking more new female authors, especially those of women's suspense fiction.

> *Women buy 75% to 80% of new fiction. Publishers like to try to capitalize on this market.*

Nancy's novel was perfect! I decided to submit the manuscript simultaneously to fourteen hardcover and hard-soft publishers whom I thought would be interested. (Fourteen is my lucky number.) Because I had been in the business for so long, I had established relationships with many senior editors, so I tried to select the editors I thought would fall in love with the project. On a Tuesday in February, fourteen manuscripts were hand-delivered. That Thursday, I was in Fort Worth to celebrate my father-in-law's birthday and to host a luncheon for sixty Texas authors. On Friday, I phoned the office and learned that I had received a phone call from a major New York publisher regarding *Mitigating Circumstances*. There was no indication of the editor's interest, so I called her. She told me that when her lunch was canceled the day before, she stayed in the office and read Nancy's manuscript—she couldn't put it down! There were a few minor problems but she wanted to buy it. And, she wanted to make a deal to include Nancy's second—and at that time unfinished—novel, *Prince of the Oaks*. In representational terms, this was a minor miracle! Not only had an actual editor read the manuscript (not a reader or assistant), but that editor was willing to make an offer for—not one but—two books! As you may imagine, I was tremendously excited by this turn of events, but I had thirteen other phone calls to make, to see if the other publishers were equally interested.

On Monday, back in New York, I received a call from Michaela Hamilton, Editorial Director of New American Library's mass-market lines (it's now Dutton-Signet, a division of Penguin Putnam). She wanted to acquire another book I represented, called *The Secrets of Seduction*, by Brenda Venus. I was happy about that but I also wanted to know her interest in the sizzling women's suspense thriller for which I believed I would receive an offer from a different publisher the next day. I then called the remaining publishers. (Although the manuscript had been in the marketplace for only several days, and I didn't want to appear pushy, I had to kindle their interest in it.) Early Tuesday morning,

Michaela Hamilton had phoned three times: she wanted to buy the Brenda Venus book—and both of Nancy's books!

I decided to take Nancy's books to auction, with an established bid of $600,000 for a two-book, hard-soft world rights deal. I set an auction date, offering NAL, the floor holder, a 5% topping privilege. The phones didn't stop ringing—and not just from New York but from Hollywood producers, too. Publishers offered a whopping $750,000 for two books, hardcover rights only. NAL exercised its 5% topping right and we ended up placing Nancy's two books for $787,500. Simultaneously, Tri Star Pictures, a division of Sony Corporation, offered to option the feature film rights for $125,000, against a high six-figure sum, outbidding all other interested film companies.

> One reason Tri Star Pictures paid so much money for the film rights is because director Jonathan Demme (Silence Of The Lambs, Philadelphia) wanted to direct it through his Clineca Estetico Productions, which was based at Tri Star. The film rights were purchased; the film is still in development. Demme's company and Tri Star still hold the rights to Mitigating Circumstances. Director Agnieszka Holland (Europa, Europa, The Secret Garden) has co-written the screenplay with Jean-Yves Pitoun and Sean Slovo and Agnieszka is slated to direct the movie.

This episode turned out to be the beginning of Nancy Taylor Rosenberg's publishing career. One publisher offered NAL $500,000 for a floor bid to the paperback rights to the two books. But NAL executives didn't want to sell the paperback rights and asked me to consider a four-book, hard-soft deal with them. Nancy agreed to the deal. I wound up negotiating a four-book, hard-soft multi-million dollar contract for Nancy, loaded with what I call "bells and whistles."

> *When a publisher really wants an author, or a particular book, it is willing to make large concessions in the contract, which is a rare occurrence. The contract we negotiated for Nancy is filled with the following phrase: "Not to be considered a precedent."*

Nancy Rosenberg is published in over twenty-eight countries. The first four books of this contract—*Mitigating Circumstances, Interest of Justice, First Offense* and *Trial by Fire* were all *New York Times* paperback best-sellers. I also placed *California Angel,* Nancy's next book; this, too, became a *New York Times* bestseller. I then negotiated a second four-book contract for Nancy at a substantially higher advance guarantee than her first. These events evolved into what I call, "Wonderful Circumstances."

I sincerely hope that someone who reads this book will create a book as "red-hot" as *Mitigating Circumstances* and that I'll be able to represent him. Then, the next time I update this book, I can write another chapter called, "More Wonderful Circumstances."

"Bear in mind that just because you have a gimmick doesn't mean you are going to get representation."

—*PM*

CHAPTER FIVE

SPECIALTY BOOKS

"Most writers regard the truth as their most valuable possession, and therefore are most economical in its use."
—Mark Twain

Many years ago, there was a book published called *Real Men Don't Eat Quiche*. It was extremely successful and was the seminal book of a genre called the *Non-book,* or *Specialty Book*—that which is not considered a serious book.

A Non-book or Specialty Book is still categorized as a book because it is published material between two covers.

Are you aware of a Non-book called The Nothing Book. *The perfect example of a Non-book, it consisted of a black binder with blank pages in-between. It sold millions of copies.*

There are various categories of Non-books, or Specialty Books, including humor (Erma Bombeck), cartoon (the Garfield series, anything by Charles M. Schultz) and gimmick (*Real Men Don't Eat Quiche*) and a book of lists (rationalizations for women who do too much work while running with the wolves). Unbelievably, these publishing programs have become extremely successful. Think about it: Every time a new fad is created or a new invention hits the market, there is the possibility for a new kind of Non-book.

> *When telephone answering machines first became popular, publishers everywhere were producing a telephone answering machine book, complete with examples of messages you could leave on your machine and how to play practical jokes on friends utilizing them. My agency represented a book called* At the Sound of the Beep. *It included humorous anecdotes about the use of a telephone answering machine.*

It may seem to you that joke books have been on the up-swing, but they have been a staple of Specialty Books for perhaps a century.

> *Every manifestation of joke book has been published, from* Truly Tasteless Jokes *to* Gross Jokes *to* The Worst Jokes You Have Ever Heard *to a series called* Joking Off. *Some of these joke book series have been published in numerous volumes and continue to be staples of publishing.*

Now, you're probably wondering whether or not you should write a Non-book or a Specialty Book. My advice to you is to consider this very carefully. It's easy to imagine the success you might have publishing a book that sells 100,000+ copies. But, finding the right gimmick and the right publisher is not easy.

> *Not so long ago, the* Questions *books had been successful and, as a result, I received a number of proposals for similar books; none has been placed.*

Research the marketplace carefully before considering the development of any Specialty project. Just because you have a gimmick doesn't mean you're going to sell it. Many agencies may have the same philosophy we do: we represent *authors*—professional writers with long-term careers ahead of them—not one-shot wonders.

"Strange as it may seem, beginning screenwriters may have a better chance at getting produced if they adapt their unproduced screenplay into a book."

—*PM*

CHAPTER SIX

HOW TO SELL YOUR WRITING FOR FEATURE FILMS OR TELEVISION

*You call this a script? Give me a couple of $5,000
a week writers and I'll write the script myself.*
—Joe Pasternak

One of the greatest pleasures an author can experience is having his work published. And, when the manuscript metamorphoses into the visual image—thereby reaching a far greater audience—the author's pleasure and monetary reward increase substantially. I'm proud to say that the works of many of our clients have made the transition from written word to film. Unfortunately, as difficult as it is to place a manuscript with a publisher, the process of selling a screenplay, a television script or the film rights to a book is even more difficult. The reason is simple: books may cost thousands of dollars to publish, but movies cost millions of dollars to produce. If publishing is a jungle, the movie business is a jungle on another planet!

In the field of television, approximately five percent of the scripts controlled by major television networks reach production. The percentage for features is lower. Film and television executives look at books—all books, regardless how prestigious or obscure they may be—as raw material for their movie-making machines. In fact, they are bombarded with so much material (books, scripts, plays, etc.), they often become inured to the mystique presented by a really good book. Unlike publishers (who buy a manuscript they love and baby it through publication), producers are not always so committed to a project they fall in love with. Producers may buy a project because it's "hot" (i.e., topical) or because it's perfect for an actor they want to work with. But, what if the subject or the actor cools? The project is shelved. Some projects are bought with every intention of being made; others are purchased so no one else will have the story. As pessimistic as this sounds, an upside exists: there is an ever-growing demand for new product to feed to theaters, television and cable, and to the pay-per-view and videocassette markets. And, this is good for writers.

There are a number of ways a writer can increase the chances of successfully moving his work off the page and onto the screen. The most important thing to do is obtain representation, which is crucial at this juncture. A good representative should have valuable contacts in the film and television industries; in addition, he should be knowledgeable about which networks or studios are buying new properties and, especially, what KIND they're buying. (For example, several years ago, Turner Network Television [TNT] recently began producing original programming; suddenly, there was a new entity in the marketplace—and an alternative to the three major networks—where a writer could sell his material.) For the writer whose representative is aware of the various nuances of Hollywood (which executives are where; which network is looking for what kind of property, etc.) a sale can be made easily and swiftly. Additionally, a good representative will know intimately about the development process and how to present properties to the appropriate actors, directors or production companies. A positive response from a "name talent" will prove the property's viability to studio executives and, thus make the sale that much easier.

Representatives involved with Hollywood often spend as much of their time "packaging" projects (matching director, actors, and other talent, to a script) as they do selling scripts.

FINDING AN AGENT

There is no easy way for an aspiring writer to find representation, but you can start by doing one of the following:
- Contact the Writers Guild of America (WGA)[4] and request from them a list of agencies that will read unsolicited materials from new writers.
- Consult many of the well-known writer reference books (Writer's Market; Literary Marketplace; Jeff Herman's Writer's Guide to Book Editors, Publishers, and Literary Agents; Lone Eagle Publishing's Film Producers, Studios, Agents and Casting Directors Guide and Film Writers Guide, etc.), which list agents and managers and the types of writing they represent.

Do not approach a representative with your work until you are absolutely certain you are ready to be represented.

---

4. There are Writers Guild branches in Los Angeles, New York and London.

Agents are not editors or teachers—they are dealmakers. Your understanding and respect of their function are necessary elements in any potential writer/agent relationship.

Before signing with an agent, you must ascertain whether or not he or she has the contacts necessary to represent your work successfully. For example, most traditional New York literary representatives do not directly handle film or television writers, nor do they represent their own writers when the book rights of one of their projects is sold to film or TV; instead, they have ties to West Coast reps who handle the sales for them, splitting the commission on those rights. Conversely, there are reps who work only in film and television with "sister" agencies in New York to handle the publishing side for their clients. And, some representatives, of which I am one, have connections on both the East and West Coasts and are comfortable closing the sale of both literary and film properties.

When searching for a representative, consider the following:

- Find out the number (and type) of film and/or television, or literary, deals the representative has already made;
- Ascertain whether the agent has continuing buyer and client relationships (speak to some of his clients, if you can).
- Ask if the representative is skilled in the areas of negotiation, rights and contracts.
- Try to determine if the agent is interested only in a specific project you have written or if he will work with you as a writer on developing your career.

In addition, you want someone who will stick with you through your dry periods—and not just during those times when your work is selling (all professional writers know there are dry periods during a career).

Selecting the appropriate representative depends upon your goals as a writer. If you are primarily interested in writing a book, with the possibility of developing a screenplay from it some time in the future, a New York literary representative is probably your best option. If your primary interest is writing for film or TV, a West Coast representative is preferable.

> *It is my opinion that, during the next few years, a greater consolidation of these two fields of representation will occur, just as we have seen mergers between publishing and film companies which have resulted in huge media conglomerates.*

As the proliferation of media giants continues to occur, writers will need to be especially vigilant in protecting their work. Therefore, it is crucial that your representative believes in you and your work.

USING AN ATTORNEY

You can retain an attorney to represent your material. An attorney who specializes in entertainment or contract law should be able to negotiate a solid contract, which would put you at a decided advantage. However, while your contract might be well-drawn, there is no guarantee that all the provisions regarding subsidiary rights licenses and other aspects of that contract are good. Also, your attorney may not have a thorough knowledge of the ins and outs (including the players) of the marketplace. This can be reflected in the length of time an attorney takes to negotiate a simple deal. A literary representative is in the marketplace on a daily basis and therefore may be able to better expedite a sale.

It's the agent's job to know the trends and the players of the industry. And, few attorneys have the time or the inclination to watch the business as closely as an agent.

Bear in mind that, unlike representatives, many attorneys do not work on a commission basis, so there could be the specter of a substantial legal bill when the contract is completed. If you are using an attorney to negotiate your contract:

- Try to predetermine the legal costs;
- Negotiate these costs with the attorney prior to hiring him.

Attorneys in the film and television industries who don't work on commission generally may negotiate to work for a percentage (typically, five percent of the writer's fee) or on a retainer.

SELLING YOUR PROJECT

Strange as it may seem, a novice screenwriter may have a better chance of getting his script produced if he adapts his unproduced project into a book. If the book is published, it can be optioned and then adapted into a screenplay—with a studio's input and at the studio's expense. The motion picture, television and cable industries purchase the rights to hundreds of books every year (especially best-sellers) in their search for new material.

Made-for-television projects generally cost less to produce than what it costs a network to broadcast a major theatrical film, so television, particularly, likes to look to publishing as a source for story ideas.

A book that already has been published and has found an audience obviously has an advantage over an unproduced screenplay that has been making the studio rounds for awhile.

Besides screenplays, film studios look to all traditional sources for their film projects, including books (Jurassic Park, The Hunt for Red October), *stage plays* (Marvin's Room, A Few Good Men), *or musicals* (Evita, A Chorus Line).

Book authors should realize that roughly 100,000 books are published in this country every year but, worldwide, only approximately 1,000 movies (including movies-of-the-week and cable movies) are made. The odds are not in the writer's favor, but trying to sell a project is certainly worth a try because the rewards can be phenomenal.

Lawyer-turned-novelist Scott Turow received $1 million for the film rights to Presumed Innocent, *his first book; Warren Adler, author of* The War of the Roses, *scored a record-breaking $1.2 million for the rights to his next novel. And, Grisham and Crichton have broken the $5 million mark more than once with* A Time To Kill *and* Jurassic Park/Lost World *respectively.*

THE METAMORPHOSIS OF BOOK TO SCREEN

The art of dramaturgy—writing a play, a screenplay, a television movie, or a miniseries—is very specific and vastly different from the art of writing prose. Simply stated, not all authors are suited to adapting their own books, nor do they wish to.

> *"It was like passing a scene of a highway accident and being relieved to learn that nobody had been seriously injured,"* responded author Martin Cruz Smith, when asked how he liked the movie version of his novel Gorky Park.

First off, when the rights to a book are sold, the studio, network or producer has the right to change it without approval from the author. If this happens, it's often because the purchaser is unwilling to let the author write the screenplay; sometimes, it is felt that the screenplay should veer drastically away from the source material. If you have strong feelings about these issues (i.e., adapting the work yourself; guarding against major changes, etc.), you should consider these elements prior to selling your work. It is important for you to know what you want when selling the rights to your work. Your feelings will determine the exact form of the deal, including who will be able to purchase the rights (if there is more than one bidder). For example, if you're interested in a second career as a screenwriter, you might take less money for the book rights in exchange for a deal to write the script. Other permutations are possible.

Have you read William Goldman's *Adventures in the Screen Trade*.[5] Goldman provides an excellent example of a book author who has adapted his novels into screenplays (i.e., *The Princess Bride, Marathon Man, Magic*) and has found success in Hollywood.[6]

---

5. Goldman, William. *Adventures in the Screen Trade: A Personal View of Hollywood and Screenwriting*. New York: Warner Books, Inc., 1983.

6. Goldman won an Academy Award for Best Screenplay in 1969, for *Butch Cassidy And The Sundance Kid*; and he won an Academy Award in 1976, for Best Adapted Screenplay (*All The President's Men*).

> *Goldman's fees range upwards of a million dollars per script, although it took him years to reach such heights. Of course, if you are William Goldman, John Grisham or Michael Crichton—in other words, your name is synonymous with "success"—you can write your own ticket.*

Sometimes, the author is not the only person who controls the rights to a story. This is particularly true in works of nonfiction. My client Steve Salerno wrote *Deadly Blessing*, a true crime book about a bizarre murder in Texas. The book was eagerly pursued by a number of television production companies before it was sold to David L. Wolper Productions, a producer for Warner Bros. Television. An Errors and Omissions Policy (requested by networks when dealing with a work of nonfiction) was taken out with an insurance company. This expensive document protects the network from litigation in case someone involved in the case should sue the network for libel or defamation of character. Warner Bros. soon realized that Vicky Daniel, one of the principals involved in the case, had NOT agreed to sell HER rights to the story. So, for *Deadly Blessing*, Warner Bros. purchased ALL court transcripts: 16,000 pages, at $1.50 per page. The transcripts were used as background material by the screenwriter, John Ireland. With the E&O policy in place, the production company proved it acted in reasonable "good faith" and with "due diligence" to produce a realistic version of a story that was in the public domain. Without Warner Bros.' willingness to invest its money at this early stage—before the script was written—the project would not have gotten off the ground.

The resulting script was actually very sympathetic to Vicky Daniel; the project was produced and aired on ABC television under the title, A Bed of Lies *(aired January 1992).*

BREAKING INTO TELEVISION

Sometimes, an unproduced writer can break into television by writing a *Treatment* (an outline of a story) for a movie or a proposed series rather than a full-length *Teleplay*. The reason for this is simple: if the idea is a good one, the producer will buy the story idea from you (thus, your break into television) and then hire an established television writer to adapt your idea into a teleplay. Writing for television sounds easier than it is (due to the necessity of writing for commercial breaks), and it is why producers and networks can be uneasy with new writers. Usually, television networks have strict criteria for hiring writers, so a novice writer will need to prove his worth to those in television.

Experienced TV writers understand that TV movies are interrupted by twelve to fourteen minutes of commercial time per hour and usually are adept at designing scripts with "cliffhangers" before each break. They manage to retain the story's basic integrity and continuity despite the constant breaks.

A treatment, no matter how brief, is evidence that a writer can write. The producer may not be sold on your story, but he may be impressed enough with your writing ability to hire you for a different project.

In both film and television, it is essential to sell the writer over the project, especially since it is common for a property to take years to reach completion.

Treatments usually run between eight and fifteen double-spaced pages and include a full synopsis of the story. There are no other hard-and-fast rules as to what else should be included in the package.

If your treatment is, say, a true crime story for a TV Movie of the Week, you may wish to supplement the synopsis with some well-chosen newspaper articles illustrating the widespread interest in your subject. Or, if the project is a straight drama, you might want to break down the idea into separate acts to exhibit the strength of the story's dramatic structure. If your idea is a comedy, include sample dialogue to prove that you can write funny lines.

Some treatments include descriptions of the main characters so the producer can imagine actors appropriate for the roles. (Sometimes, reference is made to a well-known actor: " . . . This character is a Clint Eastwood type . . .").

When writing a treatment, you should make it as powerful and eloquent as possible. But, a treatment is only as good as the screenplay that will follow. I once placed a prominent author's work with a network days after I secured the publishing rights for his book—and the book wasn't written at the time. The entire deal was based on a nine-page treatment. In this case, the key was the involvement of a "prominent author." (This same author sold his next book as a miniseries, also without a completed manuscript.)

A treatment is, at best, a vehicle by which a writer makes a deal to write—and not writing itself.

If your treatment is not selling, reexamine your commitment to your story idea. If you are convinced that it is THE movie you want to write, begin writing the screenplay and hope you'll sell the idea with a completed script. If you have doubts about the idea, put the treatment away, at least for a while, and begin writing something else.

If you have an idea for a television series, the best way to attract the attention of a production company or a network executive is by writing a treatment that includes an overview of the entire series, brief descriptions of the major characters, one-paragraph synopses of thirteen episodes (thirteen represents half the number of episodes for a full-season commitment from a network for any series) and perhaps a completed script of the series pilot. Be forewarned: of all the deals discussed in this book, selling a television series is the one least likely to be made. The networks receive vast numbers of proposals for series; only a few of them get to production, and most of these are from established writers, producers and stars. In fact, a 500-page book is available that offers television series concepts that reached the development stage and were not produced.[7]

One successful way of selling an idea is to keep abreast of news events. Buy the rights to someone's story and develop it into a movie or miniseries idea, write a treatment, and then, in conjunction with your representative or packager, present the proposal to a network or to an independent television producer. Networks always like to get in on the ground floor of a potentially best-selling, high-ratings idea, which is why there often is a proliferation of news stories-turned-movies, i.e., the World Trade Center bombing and the O.J. Simpson murder trial have both been subjects of recent TV movies.

---

7. *Unsold Television Pilots,* by Lee Goldberg 1955-1988. New York: McFarland. 1990

*During one week, a major publisher received four-
teen proposals for a book based on the Stuart murder in Boston; the story of a young man who murdered his pregnant wife and denied it.*

Occasionally, material strikes such a chord that a producer is willing to invest his time, energy, emotion AND
money to develop it for the screen. This happened to me
after I read an epistolary novel called, *Miss 4th of July,
Goodbye.* I optioned it with a partner. Set in a West Virginia
coal-mining town, around the turn of the century, the book
is about a young girl who defends the rights of a black man
victimized by the KKK. The story is even more poignant
because the girl, as an immigrant, is subject to bigotry herself. We submitted the book to Disney Television and received a very positive response. Just as the situation looked
promising, Disney shelved the project: it no longer was interested in historical dramas. To me, it felt like a personal
rejection. I could only imagine how the author must have
felt. However, we were fortunate because everything did turn
out for the project: it was made into a movie for the Disney
Channel, retitled, *Goodbye, Miss 4th Of July;* it starred Louis
Gossett, Jr., and Chris Sarandon, and was directed by George
Miller (*The Man From Snowy River*).

During my long association with author Vincent
Bugliosi, we worked together to see that his nonfiction book,
Till Death Us Do Part, successfully make the transition to
the screen. Published in the late 1970s, the book won the
Edgar Allan Poe Award[8] and was a hot property. But it was
rejected by nearly twenty-five producers—for any number
of slight or insignificant reasons. Vincent and I had an enormous amount invested in this book—an investment of conviction and emotion—feelings that go far beyond money.

8. The prestigious fiction or non-fiction literary award bestowed annually.

We finally sold the book to Edgar J. Scherick Productions; it was made into an NBC "Movie of the Week" starring Treat Williams. (1992, Yves Simoneon)

As an aspiring television writer, you may be tempted to write a sample script for an existing show (with hopes it will sell) to prove your ability to write episodic TV. This exercise is more futile than you might expect. (In fact, I don't recommend this option unless you live in Los Angeles and can devote your time to breaking into the business.) If you insist on this exercise, write an episode of your favorite show, but try getting it to the producers of a DIFFERENT show.

THE TELEVISION MINISERIES

Ever since *Roots* (the nonfiction book by Alex Haley that traced the author's heritage to African slaves), network television has been in love with the Miniseries (a long-form TV movie broadcast over several nights) and producers have turned to best-selling books as a source for this form of TV entertainment. *Rich Man, Poor Man; Lonesome Dove; Robin Cook's Invasion; Stephen King's The Shining*—all of these successful, popular TV miniseries were based on best-selling novels.

Helter Skelter, based on former Los Angeles District Attorney Vincent Bugliosi's book of the same name, was made into a miniseries 1976, and is a prime example of a successful television miniseries. It dealt with a sensational, true-crime story; the characters (including beautiful actors and actresses and hippies-turned-murderers) were larger than life; and it offered, through Bugliosi's point of view, some redeeming social value. Journalists and attorneys have an advantage in this area: they are often among the first to learn about interesting, marketable crime stories and, as such, they can begin developing a treatment for the idea long before other writers have heard of the case. When a true crime story cannot be found, a mutation is created: the "docudrama," a combination of fact and fiction, has become an accepted genre of the TV movie or miniseries.

AVOIDING CATCH-22

Typically, people who write for television are members of the Writers Guild of America (WGA), which means they have sold at least one script to a production company that is a WGA signatory (this includes most network shows, some syndication and some cable shows). Signatories rarely hire writers who are not members of WGA. Yes, it's a "Catch-22" situation: you can't become a member of WGA without selling a script; but you can't sell a script without being a member of WGA.

There is a chance that a producer will be so enamored of your work that he will buy your project or make a deal with you to write an episode of his show, thus allowing you to become a member of WGA at a later date—but it is a slim chance.

Success in television is difficult, but if you make it, you'll almost certainly make it big.

> *I represented a writer named David Burke, who co-wrote the pilot for a television series called* Crime Story. *Since then, he has worked his way up the TV ladder from Story Editor on the show to Executive Producer of the critically acclaimed series* Wiseguy *and* Seaquest DSV *(writing many episodes for both series as well).*

Writers Guild scale for a one-hour episode of a primetime series is around $25,000, plus a guaranteed rerun payment; and, there are potentially lucrative foreign sales possibilities (anywhere between $15,000 and $50,000)—all for a sixty-page script. Writing revenue from syndicated series can also be quite lucrative.

THE DEVELOPMENT DEAL

Once a writer sells a producer on his ability and the producer shows a desire to hire the writer, the writer's agent sets up a *development deal* with the producer. A typical development deal (for feature films or television) works like this:

- A producer options the writer's property for a set period of time, usually a year (with an opportunity to renew the option for a second year). A one-year option represents a down payment of approximately ten percent of the full purchase price of the property.

- For that year, the producer controls the property exclusively and can promote its sale (to a television network, production company or studio). If the property is purchased by the network, production company or studio, the producer recoups his option payment, along with other development costs he incurred. The author receives his full payment (the remaining ninety percent of the full purchase price) and the process of developing the script for production (either by the author or by a different screenwriter) begins.

Some prominent producers have what is known as an *output deal* with a specific network or studio; this guarantees that a certain number of their projects will be made each year.

Mike Cochran, a well-known, thirty-year veteran Associated Press reporter, and one of my former clients, published a nonfiction book called And Deliver Us From Evil, *a compilation of true crime stories set in Texas. One episode concerned an innocent man accused of murder who then became a fugitive from justice. Mike optioned the rights to this chapter to a television producer for one year; the story went into development. At the end of the first option period, the producer had not sold the story. At this point, the producer could have paid Mike the remaining purchase price to own the story outright or he could have renewed the option for another year and continued to shop it around. He renewed the option and the film was made and aired on CBS as* Fugitive Among Us.

On the positive side, there has never been such a diverse amount of material available to the viewing public. Big-budget blockbuster-type movies and miniseries always seem to find an audience. Currently, offbeat stories have a better chance of being optioned than at any other time in recent memory. A front-page headline in *Daily Variety* summed it up: "Warts and All: TV Embraces Fact and Flaws and Frailties." In the article, the author noted that the leading TV series today are shows like *Roseanne* and the *The Simpsons* which present a less-than-perfect view of contemporary America. And, look at the soaring success of *The X-Files*: viewers definitely have shown their approval of this offbeat, dark show.

Many distributors feel that the primary audience for movies is comprised of kids. Only kids, they rationalize, have the time, energy, disposable income and fanaticism necessary to see a movie seven or eight times in a theater. However, the days are past when any film set in outer space with expensive special effects is a guaranteed box-office blockbuster. The trend for popular entertainment films these days is to look for something that will appeal to kids while also keeping their parents happy. A perfect example is the Batman series of movies, films that work very hard to strike this kind of balance. Is there anything that will definitely sell? No. But lately there has been a trend in Hollywood toward more comedy films—specifically, films that mix comedy with action and more spectacular "event" films.

Any writer should be aware of the constantly changing trends in the television and film industries and should be prepared to adapt to these changes—at the drop of a hat. In fact, the writer who is truly successful in movies or TV doesn't follow the trends—he writes stories that interest him and, in the process, may SET the trends.

There is always room for a quality screenplay. Although the quality may not necessarily be recognized immediately, and it may not receive its financial due, there is a producer somewhere who is willing to make a film simply because it should be made. Many major actors now have their own production companies and make an effort to alternate between commercial and less commercial fare.

In Hollywood, the competition is fierce but the rewards can be substantial. So, go west, young writers! There's success in them thar Hollywood Hills.

"Someone will

come along and

seduce you with

their belief in

your writing."

—*PM*

CHAPTER SEVEN

PACKAGING

Did you hear about the screenwriter who submitted his first screenplay to a major studio? A week later, he received two rejection letters: one rejecting the current script; one rejecting a future script.

The entertainment industry believes it can best avoid severe financial loss by combining compatible marketing "hooks," whether they are two bankable actors; a star actor and a star musician (for the possibility of a hit movie and soundtrack); a star director and a best-selling author, etc. Should a project not do well in one area, there are other elements to pick up the slack and improve the total financial performance of an entertainment property. That's why motion picture and television deals today emphasize the *package*. A package, then, is not an afterthought or a surprising by-product of the filmmaking process. Rather, it has become the prerequisite of virtually all studio deals and the constant objective of representatives, packagers, directors, producers and would-be film investors. Indeed, some films are more famous in the industry for their packaging efforts than for their quality. *The Cable Guy* (Columbia—1996; Ben Stiller, 95 mins.) appeared to be a no-lose package, matching wildly popular comic Jim Carrey with hip, talented director Ben Stiller and popular leading man Matthew Broderick; it was a colossal bomb. An example of successful packaging is *Rain Man* (MGM/UA—1988; Barry Levinson, 128 mins.); this film was produced because of Michael Ovitz's strong belief in it. Then president of Creative Artists Agency, Ovitz packaged the film several different times and saw it through many screenplay drafts before it finally went into production. It eventually married the talents of superstar actors Dustin Hoffman and Tom Cruise with A-list director Barry Levinson.[9]

Before studios green light a project, they want to know what the package is; industry players no longer attempt to merely place the film rights to a property or sell an original screenplay—they always try to package the property.

> *As one studio executive said to me, "Peter, you always have terrific projects, but who's going to make the film? Bring me a filmmaker. Then, try to put together as complete a package as possible."*

The package may also include co-production financing or foreign pre-sales (including production financing, prints and advertising or even negotiable bank guarantees based solely on creative talent).

The average cost of a movie these days is around $40 million; many major studio films have budgets close to or above $100 million.[10] That's a lot of money to risk on unknown actors or directors. And, competition is fierce, especially when the goal is to beat the billions in worldwide revenue racked up by recent huge successes like *Jurassic Park*

---

9. *Rain Man* won Academy Awards for Best Picture, Best Director (Barry Levinson), Best Actor (Dustin Hoffman), Best Original Screenplay (Ronald Bass, Barry Morrow); and was nominated for Best Art Direction/Set Direction, Best Cinematography, Best Film Editing, Best Original Score.

10. *Titanic,* a co-production of Paramount Pictures and 20th Century Fox set for release at the end of 1997, reportedly has a budget exceeding $200 million.

and *The Lost World, Independence Day,* the *Batman* series, *Men In Black,* or the *Star Wars* trilogy. It's almost impossible to beat these juggernauts . . . unless, of course, you've got a "can't-miss" package.

The film package that begins with a best-selling book (100,000 hardcover copies sold) has an advantage. Unfortunately, very few books published in this country ever reach such sales or status. (These properties are heavily pursued and are optioned quickly by major studios, networks or well-connected independent producers—usually before they hit the printing presses.)

A more modestly successful book may still have strong screen or television potential, especially if the book contains a cinematic concept or deals with a topical subject. *Perennials*—books on subjects that are always popular, i.e., true crime—are always good projects to package. In fact, true crimes have been the rage on television for many years; most of these TV movies have been packaged around books that originally brought the crimes to national attention. However, even best-selling books cannot overcome all the obstacles inherent in the filmmaking process. The sad fact is that fewer than one out of ten books optioned by film or television producers goes into production (the odds are worse for an optioned original screenplay). Typically, the reason is because a satisfactory package could not be assembled.

An independent producer or production company—those entities which function without specific connection to a studio or network—are usually active buyers of book properties. This is especially true if an independent has a "first-look" deal with a studio. Then, the independent is compensated by the studio for the purchase of the rights and for office overhead; sometimes, the company receives base salaries against future production fees.

But, it all starts with the story: the book is a major element of any package. It is usually developed as a screenplay by the original writer or by a screenwriter brought onto the project. When the first-draft screenplay (or some written form of the material) is completed, its film potential should be self-evident. The script should be simple, concise, clear and without artistic pretension. Remember: the audience wants to see a *film*, not a photographic reproduction of the printed page.

Despite rumors to the contrary, it isn't true that producers "can't read." They simply like to prioritize their schedules. So, keep your ideas and scripts simple. Whenever I go into a meeting, I try to rehearse the pitch so that I present the property in one paragraph—two to five succinct sentences, or maybe even one (if it's a "high concept" idea).

Besides the story, all packages should have:
- A director interested in the property (it helps if he is as much a "star" as any actor).
- A "star."

Creating a package without star names is like baking bread without yeast—your project won't rise, no matter how long you bake it. If there is an extraordinary angle, i.e., a Top 10 hit song or a mass media event like the O.J. Simpson murder trial, a project could move forward without stars. But, generally, stars are tantamount to the final deal. An actor who is on the verge of stardom or a director who has made one or two critically acclaimed but small films are not significant enough to package.

In the basic law of packaging, a package is as strong as its weakest element. Any movie with A-list talent, i.e., Dustin Hoffman, Clint Eastwood, Tom Hanks, Harrison Ford, Brad Pitt, Tom Cruise, Jodie Foster, Michelle Pfeiffer, Steven Spielberg, Ron Howard, John Grisham, Michael Crichton, etc., has an excellent shot at being made. But, how often are

A-list talents available. Therefore, packaging efforts sometimes resemble sleights-of-hand. If you have two strong elements, perhaps a star actor or actress and a strong property, the package may overcome the fact that the director hasn't yet made a major film. This kind of packaging "magic" makes it an art.

The First Wives' Club (Paramount—1996; Hugh Wilson, 96 mins) was a package made in Heaven: it was based on a popular novel and starred a trio of Hollywood's hottest actresses.

Before the ink was dry on the rights to Steel Magnolias, *it was almost guaranteed a green light: it was based on a hit play, starred Academy Award-winning actresses Shirley MacLaine, Olympia Dukakis and Sally Field; country-and-western music star Dolly Parton; popular young actresses Daryl Hannah and Julia Roberts; it was to be directed by the acclaimed Herb Ross and produced by film mogul Ray Stark, who saw the potential in the play and was wise enough to purchase the rights.*

LET'S TALK MONEY

Once the talent is in place, it's time to finance the picture.

Financing without a good package is like a well without water: no matter how deep the well, it's just another hole in the ground.

When producers of a film give up their equity in it in exchange for additional financing from an outside partner, co-production financing has occurred. In this case, a partnership is created, whereby profits are split because some of the rights to the film—e.g., foreign, video, television, etc.— are pre-sold. Besides raising equity capital for production, a pre-sale may also involve a negotiable bank guarantee. When this happens, a potential buyer agrees to pay a certain amount of money when a final print of the film is available. Such a letter of commitment, combined with the filmmaker's reputation, is then used to obtain credit from a bank.

Below-the-line financing refers to production costs. Above-the-line costs are defined as those other than for the physical production, i.e., acquisition of the property, talent (director, producer and actors), etc.

What makes packaging a business—and not just an art— is the fact that a financial scheme is necessary to make the whole production click. As with everything else in Hollywood, it comes down to money: in the case of a film or television package, production costs, financing arrangements, subsidiary sales, pre-sales, escalations, step deals, videocassette advances, back-end guarantees and many other variations on the theme must be considered.

Most programming on Home Box Office (HBO) is based on a combination of financing arrangements, which makes any one of their productions a safe, almost guaranteed investment.

While many in Hollywood package deals with talent, only a few can be referred to as *packagers*—those who put the financial arrangements in place. If one of these players is on your team, it could make the difference in getting your work produced.

Since Don Quixote was not stopped by the realities of his world, packagers are likewise not intimidated by the windmills of Hollywood: it doesn't matter that they're selling a commodity that doesn't exist. Generally, packagers pre-sell certain subsidiary rights or territorial rights to the film. Before the film is completed, the packager collects money for these rights so the film can complete production. Subsidiary rights include such elements as television syndication rights, product licensing rights, videocassette rights and anything anyone else can think of: the contract could apply to rights "now known in any form, or to be invented, throughout the universe for the history of recorded time." If all goes well, your packager may manage a network or cable television pre-sale for substantial money.

The marriage of a good talent package and proper financing for an independent production is no easy task. Each element interacts with all the others until the right pieces come together.

The process of packaging is a tedious, cut-and-paste effort. This can easily take several years of work.

Therefore, a successful packager often has many of the qualities that a successful representative has, i.e., the ability to deal with people under pressure, to negotiate, to mediate and to compromise. In fact, quite a few representatives have gone on to success as packagers and/or producers. The processes are so similar, it seems almost inevitable that a representative will be drawn to the packaging process if he or she is interested in the film market. Representatives who become involved in the film industry can help push an author's career far beyond his expectations.

A FEW WORDS OF ADVICE . . .

The industry is rife with original screenplays but, unfortunately, most are not as well-written as those developed from books. If a book has gone through the New York publishing mill, it should have—at the very least—a fully developed story; Hollywood respects that. In the words of mega-producer Jerry Bruckheimer, "If it's on the manuscript page, we will put it on the stage."

As a film manager, I prefer to represent an original screenplay only as part of a package. Screenplays considered by themselves are very difficult to sell or place. And, I usually repeat the same advice to all aspiring writers: consider writing a novelized version of your screenplay to create interest in the property for packaging purposes. If the property works as a book, it has a good chance of being placed; then it's in a better position for others to evaluate its true film potential. This approach also can triple your income: you earn money from the book's publication, from the sale of the movie rights, and, one hopes, from the sale of your screenplay adaptation of it.

> *I currently represent several developed properties, new screenplays, various novelists and a few directors. The package always spurs me on. Our sister company, Infinity Management International, has grown exponentially since I joined forces with Jon Karas in November, 1996 and, as of this writing, we have signed over fifty director and screenwriter clients. We already have over a dozen films in development. Part of our success is due to our good taste in clients and our responsiveness to them and to the market. But equally important is the fact that there is real talent out there waiting to be discovered.*

Hollywood loves a good package. So if you are a writer and you want your project made into a film, find a producer (or, do it yourself) and put together a package with recognizable actors, director, etc. Then, get a distributor. You may need to negotiate pre-sales to raise production funds—hopefully you'll do this without bargaining your rights away and giving up too much too early on a good property. You should then have a viable package. If your luck holds and your team puts together a quality film, you can check out the results shortly at your local cinema.

"The miniseries has given rise to a whole new field of writing called 'faction,' 'docudrama,' or 'infotainment,' all combinations of fact and fiction."

—PM

CHAPTER EIGHT

MARKETING YOUR SCREENPLAY

An associate producer is the only guy in
Hollywood who will associate with a producer.
—Fred Allen

In my early years in the New York publishing industry, I
believed that the experience I acquired in dealing with
both publishers and writers would eventually help me if I
ever decided to become involved in the movie industry. I
was right.

Publishing and film businesses are similar: they are both
schizophrenically split between creativity and commerce.
Furthermore, my involvement with hundreds of properties
over the years has allowed me to analyze which works have
the potential to be successful films and which will probably
never make it off the page.

As of this writing, I have successfully represented and placed
more than 800 books with publishers all over the world.
Despite the fact that I've been involved in dozens of mo-
tion picture and television rights sales, options and screen-
play development deals, only eight films have been pro-

duced based on properties with which I've been involved. One was an original screenplay, The Treasure Of The Moon Goddess; *another,* We, The Jury, *was an original treatment. Several were book adaptations:* Goodbye, Miss 4th Of July, Bed Of Lies, Till Death Us Do Part, The FBI Killer *and* A Tangled Web. *And* Fugitive Among Us *was based on a chapter of a book.*

The marketability of some of these books as movie properties is often greatly increased by the author's willingness to write the screenplay adaptation. When this happens, the author and the book become something of a package which can be offered to producers—an attractive proposition because the property always feels closer to production when a screenwriter is attached. Any writer should realize, however, that even though he adapts his own work, it does not guarantee his screenplay is the draft that gets made. Producers and executives are notorious for having second thoughts—even third and fourth thoughts—about projects and often, the writer is the victim of these extra thought processes. To producers, the fact that the writer may have lived with this material for years may not be a compelling enough argument to make the property a successful movie. And, if an element of the package changes (i.e., an actor drops out or the director leaves, citing "creative differences"), the script is usually rewritten for the new elements in the package. It never hurts for the writer to be flexible to quick changes and adaptable to rewrites.

Some time ago, I took on the representation of The Strokers, *which had a limited but successful publication run in the early 1980s. The book's author was a well-known former music agent and manager who had represented a number of hit recording artists; it was his inti-*

> *mate knowledge of the industry that enabled him to write a fictionalized "insider's account" of the music business. While in the process of soliciting the sale of the movie rights to his novel, the author wrote a screenplay adaptation; this move enhanced the attractiveness of the project enormously. Potential backers could see the metamorphosis from novel to screenplay and got a good idea of how the screenplay would evolve with further rewrites. A purchase offer for the movie rights was made; the project was nearing production when the company went out of business. The author was paid for options and screenwriting. Without his commitment to the project, his book would not have reached the pre-production stage so quickly.*

So many writers want to break into the business that screenplays often are written at no cost to the producer (these are called *spec scripts*); the writer hopes his script will sell or perhaps he'll win an assignment as a result of the exposure his writing received on the spec market. For members of the Writers Guild of America, the minimum fee for a screenplay of a medium-budgeted film is approximately $40,000+, while the payment for a low-budget feature film would be roughly 60% of that.

> *I negotiated the option for* The Killer's Game, *a novel written by Jay Bonansigna (Simon & Schuster, March, 1997); it was purchased by Andrew Lazar's production company, Mad Chance. Andrew developed the script with screenwriter Rand Ravich. When the script was sold, Ravich received a $700,000 payday, and Bonansigna gets his payday when the film is made, hopefully in early 1998.*

Many beginning screenwriters try to sell their ideas via the treatment to save themselves the time and angst of writing a full-length screenplay. Treatments usually sell for less money than a full-length screenplay. And, treatments do not always exhibit the writer's talent.

> *The best way to sell a treatment is to package the story idea with an appropriate writer and develop a first-draft screenplay. Then, try to sell this quality product to a production company or studio.*

First-time screenwriters with completed screenplays are in a stronger position to make a sale than those with a treatment or idea.

> *One of my clients, Paul Davids, finished his adventure-fantasy,* Starry Night, *before attempting to sell it. (The premise centered on Vincent van Gogh returning 100 years after his death to avenge the wrongs done to him when he was alive.) The project was optioned to an Australian film producer; when it lapsed, it was picked up by William Dear, who directed* Harry And The Hendersons *(Universal—1987; 111 mins) and* Wild America *(Warner Bros.—1997; 106 mins). The project is still in development as a major motion picture, largely because of the author's indefatigable efforts to continually improve his story.*

The screenwriter, like the novelist or the playwright or any artist, should realize that no screenplay is ever truly finished; changes will be made throughout the production and sometimes even into post-production.

> *The axiom that the screenplay is just the blueprint for the film is undeniably true.*

In your attempt to write the best screenplay possible, check out the excellent books available on plot construction, dramaturgy and the art of screenwriting. Keep in mind the bottom line: your writing must be entertaining.

I highly recommend all of Linda Seger's books on writing, including, Making A Good Script Great; *and I strongly suggest Chris Vogler's* The Writer's Journey.

Your screenplay must involve the reader to the fullest degree. For that reason, I prefer to read scripts that aren't cluttered with camera direction or lengthy descriptions; in the best-written scripts, the screenwriter takes into account the special rhythms of filmmaking. To keep your screenplay compelling, you must constantly ask yourself if your story will be of interest to anyone other than you or your immediate family. Plot, character development, visual details— all of these elements must be juggled constantly in order for a successful screenplay to result. While producers may open hundreds of screenplays, only those screenplays which grab and hold the reader's attention are read to the final page.

I met a police officer who served as a consultant on several films, including Beverly Hills Cop *(Paramount—1984; Martin Brest, 105 mins.),* Beverly Hills Cop 2 *(Paramount—1987; Tony Scott, 103 mins.), and* The Presidio *(Paramount—1988; Peter Hyams, 97 mins.). Because he worked full-time for the Los Angeles County Sheriff's Office, screenwriting was his hobby. But, he was vastly interested in improving his hobby. He came to me with his first completed screenplay; I gave him advice on how to improve it. He acted on the criticism, writing several subsequent drafts. Because of his tireless efforts, we were able to option the script to Five Rivers Productions.*

If you aspire to be a screenwriter, you should look upon your work as a process that will come to fruition over time—perhaps a long time.

> *One screenwriter we worked with put his first screenplay through five rewrites before we would submit it for him. It was sent to twenty-five producers; it was rejected by all of them. The twenty-sixth submission hit the mark: the screenplay was optioned and is in development.*

Even if you are extraordinarily fortunate and sell your first screenplay, it might be a long time (maybe even years) before it reaches the screen. Remember: every piece of writing in circulation that carries your name is establishing you as a writer in the minds of those who read it. Therefore, be certain that every piece of your writing is your absolute best effort. If you think seeing your name in print is exciting, wait until you see it on the screen.

"Your book is a

major element of

the package."

—*PM*

CHAPTER NINE

THE EPISODIC TELEVISION SERIES

Television has proved that people will look
at anything rather than at each other.
—Ann Landers

Television is big business. Unlike other facets of the entertainment industry, where it seems only the producers or studios see any profit, television offers numerous opportunities for gifted writers to receive lucrative rewards for their efforts. TV writers can be remunerated for:

- original treatments;
- series proposals;
- teleplays.

In addition, they receive residuals from royalties, foreign sales and from the rerun and syndication markets. Times have never been this good for the writer who specializes in television.

The Writers Guild of America reports that the highest amount ever recorded—$127 million— in royalties and residuals was paid to its members in the calendar year of 1996—the highest quarter in its sixty-three-year existence.

To participate in this payday, you first must break into the business. This is not a simple ambition. However, the advantage all writers have is that television is renowned for being a writer's medium: it has a voracious appetite for writing, particularly good writing. For example, the normal pickup for sitcoms and dramatic series is twenty-two; some series sell for longer terms (i.e., *3rd Rock From The Sun, Beverly Hills 90210* each had multiyear renewals). It is commonplace for a show to have several writers working on each episode, another benefit for writers.

A writer entering TV should understand certain basic rules. Good writing in episodic television is defined as that which:

- faithfully remains within the confines of its genre;
- provides a plot easily grasped within the first few minutes of the show;
- features strong, dynamic roles for the program's stars.

Good episodic television writing is NOT subtle. Perhaps more than any other kind of writing mentioned in this book, television writing is a mechanized process; it does not pay to become too attached to it or to be too experimental. The bulk of episodic television programming is comprised of stalwart cop or medical dramas or family comedies—writing that is not likely to challenge the writer's deepest resources. However, in response to the burgeoning cable market, the networks are attempting to push the button on standard TV fare. Thus, shows like *Ellen, Bronx South* or *NYPD Blue,* which traditionally would have been considered too radical for mainstream television, are being produced.

CABLE AND SYNDICATION

For the writers who do not wish to explore the network television arena, there are other markets, the most high-profile of which are cable and syndication. The cable industry has undergone an unprecedented expansion and continues to grow. Specialty programming prevails in cable, as there are channels devoted to history, biography, children's programming, etc. A writer's prospects in this area are difficult to ascertain since the possibility of finding work is dependent upon his ability to fit these specialized needs.

Ironically, the new writer's best opportunity for breaking into cable TV is probably by writing shows resembling those found on network TV! HBO, for example, began solely as a movie channel, but now it initiates a large amount of original programming, mostly in the form of TV movies or miniseries. USA Cable continually produces original "made-for-cable" movies—all in the $2.5 million range. The chances of winning a writing assignment on a cable series may be slight, but overall, there are more opportunities to get involved on the movie or miniseries fronts than ever before.

Again, it's best to have a completed screenplay or teleplay that can be used as a calling card. Then, make sure your representative is knocking on the right doors, i.e., executives who can green light a picture or a producer who can hire you to write an episode for his show.

Syndication television originated because broadcasters soon realized that there are more programming hours in the day for which any network can program. When local television stations (circa 1950) found that producing their own programming was prohibitively expensive, a syndication market of low-cost programming (such as game shows and talk shows) that could be sold to stations around the country began to surface. The syndication market has not significantly changed. Original programming that goes into syndication today is still low in cost, often being limited to one set and a host (think of any game show or even a high-end syndicated show like *America's Most Wanted*). Virtually all of these shows are produced by independent production companies which utilize a staff of writers.

The secret to breaking into network, cable and syndication, then, becomes similar to breaking into other areas of writing—create the circumstances for your own employment. In other words, create a proposal for a program that is not just viable but that also demonstrates your ability to write. Most independent production companies (television or feature) have a development department. Getting in the door to see a development person at a cable or syndicated channel often is easier than at the networks. In addition, they are usually more inclined to listen to new ideas: independents are always striving to find the next big project.

In Appendix C, No. 1, you'll find my own co-attempt at creating a syndicated series. *True Murder Mysteries* is a project I developed with Vincent Bugliosi. Conceived as a half-hour or hour-long weekly series, the show is intended to feature America's most famous murder cases during the last century; Bugliosi would be narrator and host. Once we had a proposal that we felt accurately represented our project, we enhanced its marketability by creating a "presentation script" (See Appendix C, No. 1). This script would make the show a reality in the minds of the producers we were pitching. (Our efforts always made it seem as if the program already existed; the next step was getting it on the air.) The concept sold but it has yet to be made.

Here's another rule for this business that can't be stressed too often: Just because you sell a property, it doesn't mean it will be produced. Prepare to have your heart broken many times before seeing your ambitions realized.

A proposal for a dramatic television series is included in Appendix C, No. 3. Called *The Inside Man*, it is written by Jerry Schmetterer, a well-known newspaper and television journalist. This proposal includes a treatment for the two-hour movie that would serve as a "back-door" pilot (i.e., the movie would stand alone or it would set up the series by being its first episode).

Off-network syndication programming is area of television syndication that generates tremendous sums money. Popular TV series, like *Seinfeld* or *Frasier*, go into syndication after they have aired on network television, often selling for over $1 million per episode. With little in the way of overhead or production costs to weigh it down, the show earns nearly 100% profit throughout its syndicated run. For example, *The Cosby Show* earned approximately half a billion dollars upon its initial availability for off-network syndication. With money in this range, even the writers—usually Hollywood's low men on the totem pole as far as profit participation goes—have reason to smile.

Remember the golden rule for all writers in Hollywood: **pitch yourself as well as your project.** The project could be forgotten tomorrow; make sure YOU'RE not.

"To keep your writing arresting, you must constantly ask yourself if what you are writing will be of interest to someone other than you and your immediate family."

—PM

CHAPTER TEN

CONTRACTS

Good swiping is an art in itself.
—Jules Pfeiffer

It would be a pleasure if the major concern of the movie and publishing industries was to see that a writer reaches the widest possible audience by writing in the format that is most appropriate to his work. Unfortunately, this is not the case. The concern that dominates both industries is *The Deal*—negotiating the deal, writing the contract for the deal, and, sometimes, breaking the deal. Throughout this book, I have attempted to offer you advice on how to develop your writing so that its fullest potential—in the appropriate medium—is realized.

Now, let's take a leap of faith: let's assume you have written a book or screenplay that is generating interest from professionals.

While not trying to sound negative, one must be realistic: millions of manuscripts are written each year while only approximately 100,000 books are published. Some manuscripts are immediately locked in their authors' attics; others make the rounds of agents, publishers or lawyers without success; a few appear on the marketplace. The numbers are worse for screenplays making the rounds in the film industry.

You might expect this to be the time to sit back and relax and wait for the kudos and financial rewards to start rolling in. NO! As a writer, you are responsible for your work and this, in turn, means you must make sure that you negotiate a quality contract for yourself.

A contract is more than a schedule of potential royalty payments or a way to ensure that you have enough copies of your book to hand out to friends. A contract is the writer's *only assurance* that his work will reach the public in the form in which he envisioned it. Of course, money is important— as a representative, I'm not going to deny that!—but self-respect is just as important.

In the author's first deal—whether it is a contract for a magazine article, short story, book or screenplay—he should expect that his work will not be sold for the optimum price. There are exceptions, of course, and stories about those twenty-five-year-old waiters who sell their first scripts for an extraordinary amount of money are well-known. It is much more likely that producers or publishers will try to take advantage of the writer's eagerness to make that first sale. (Indeed, many will attempt to take advantage of the second- or third-time writer, too.) The Cardinal Rule is to make sure that you emerge from the negotiations with a satisfactory contract. By the same token, once your book or screenplay is a smashing success, don't expect to renegotiate the deal.

CONTRACT DELICACIES

When the delicacies of negotiations come in to play, the prospective earnings of the book must be balanced against the writer's status. Many times, because the producer has acquired a terrific script by a first-time writer for an astoundingly small sum of money, the writer (motivated by his natural desire to make up for the last injustice) is able to command a huge salary for his second script (which may be nowhere near the same high quality). In fact, this is one of the principal reasons why costs in the film industry are sky-rocketing: almost nothing sold is bought on its own merits. Representatives are aware of this situation and will move to take advantage of it; it's not the healthiest course for the industry.

In publishing, certain standard royalties are offered to authors, depending on the type of book that has been written. Usually, hardcover royalties are 10% of retail earnings for the first 5,000 copies, and escalate to 15% thereafter. However, publishers sometimes lower this percentage rate on books they feel may have problems selling; sometimes, sliding rates are arranged (i.e., 10% on the first 15,000 copies; 12.5% on the next 10,000; 15% thereafter). The permutations are endless.

With simple math, you'll see that these percentages can escalate into thousands of dollars if the book is successful; if the book is not successful, the returns are minimal.

The book industry is conservative with its accounting methods. For instance, too many publishers offer a flat 6% or 7.5% royalty schedule on trade paperbacks when there might be a more imaginative way for a deal to be structured between author and publisher. I always try to negotiate higher royalties for my clients.

Representatives and authors have a symbiotic relationship: the representative is the author's employee. Only when the author's book is sold does the representative make any money. If the author's book becomes a bestseller, the representative can expect his commission to swell appreciably the next time he negotiates for that writer.

Book deals are never made on the basis of net proceeds (i.e., profits returned after the publisher has deducted its sales discounts on the book) because the success of any given project is so uncertain.

> *I represented an unauthorized biography of a well-known political figure and this book served as an exception to the net proceeds rule. Time was of the essence in publishing this book, so my client was willing to consider an unprecedented offer in order to time its publication with an important upcoming election. I negotiated a royalty for the author which began at 15% on the net proceeds for the first 5,000 copies; 17.5% on the next 5,000; 20% on everything over that. Because of the unmitigated confidence we had that the book would sell well, we structured this unusual deal; with a less certain project, I would have rejected this contract out of hand. Because the author was flexible and willing to step outside of convention, he earned considerably greater royalties than he would have with a standard publishing deal.*

Another standard of publishers that is completely outdated yet continues to exist is their attempt to maintain participation in the motion picture or television rights to the books they publish. This is a complicated and often nasty procedure in which the publisher collects a fee from the movie or television sale of one of their properties but then refuses to allow the author's revenue to "flow through" the book until they conduct their biannual accounting. (Flow-through occurs when an author's advance payments have been earned and the publisher pays the author his additional subsidiary rights earnings as they are received.) Because of this antiquated process, the author often is deprived of the returns from a legitimate sale of his book for up to six months —simply so the publisher can ensure its 10% cut. The system is unfair, but it remains in use.

I often argue for a "flow-through" clause in book contracts: once the author's advance has been paid by royalties from the sale of his book, any revenue received by the publisher should flow through to the author within ten to thirty days of its receipt.

Another common publishing practice is the publisher's attempt to claim as much as 50% of the sale of foreign rights of an author's work. A more reasonable standard, and one which I try to negotiate, is 25%. A representative can help segregate the ownership of foreign rights from the sale of the U.S. rights (which sometimes includes Canada), thereby allowing authors to increase their revenue by selling rights to publishers in individual territories, rather than seeing everything sold off in one large deal.

Should you opt not to employ a representative, please use an attorney to negotiate your contracts. Before doing so, however, review the costs involved, as it is possible to build up enormous legal fees (which sometimes would be greater than a representative's commission) for the performance of relatively simple duties.

If you choose to have an agent represent you, it could result in a long-lasting relationship with major benefits for both of you. Besides selling your writing and negotiating the contracts, your representative collects monies owed to you. Book contracts tend to be more standardized than those in the film or television industries, so collecting on royalties is generally not a problem. However, film deals are often complicated and messy, especially when net profit participation is included. Studio bookkeeping is quite labyrinthine; the writer usually stands little chance of seeing money from his points in profit participation unless he brings a lawsuit.

A well-known example of collecting—or trying to collect—on net profit participation is the Art Buchwald case against Paramount Pictures. He received a certain percentage of the net profits from Coming To America *(Paramount—1988; John Landis, 116 mins.) after he filed a lawsuit alleging that his story treatment was used as the premise for the film. After winning the lawsuit, his problem became collecting the money owed him. Despite the fact that* Coming To America *was a huge success, Paramount's books claimed otherwise.*

- Question: "Do you know what the difference between gross profit and net profit is in Hollywood?" Answer: "No profit."

To insure against this sort of accounting sleight-of-hand, I attempt to negotiate for my clients the same level of profit participation as the producer of the project. The purpose is obvious: it's harder to cheat two people out of the monies owed them than it is to cheat one, especially if they have exactly the same deal. This is known as a "Favored Nations" profit participation clause, whereby no one else involved with the production receives a more favorable definition of profits than you. In the process, the structure of the deal encourages honesty.

Any representative who manages that has done his job.

The following is a short-form deal memo for a rights option agreement on a book property that I negotiated. This kind of memo could be used for a feature film or television property. This was a fair deal for the property this contract was negotiated for.

May 20, 199_

Peter Miller, President

PMA Literary and Film Management, Inc.

132 West 22nd Street - 12th Floor

New York, NY 10011

　　　　　RE:　　Ms. Author

　　　　　　　　Mr. Author

　　　　　　　　"Working Title"

Gentleman:

　　This will confirm the agreement for an option to purchase all motion picture and television rights with respect to the book (excluding the story entitled "The New Connection") written by Ms. Author and Mr. Author entitled "Working Title."

Our agreement is as follows:

　　Ms. Author and Mr. Author have granted Producer an exclusive one year option commencing on May 16, 199_, and continuing through and including May 15, 199_, to purchase the motion picture and television rights to the book, for the total sum of Fifteen Thousand Dollars ($15,000).

　　"The Company" aka "Producer" shall have the right to extend the exclusive option period for an additional year for the additional sum of Fifteen Thousand Dollars ($15,000).

　　The purchase price for the motion picture and television rights to this prop-

erty shall be the sum of One Hundred Twenty-
five Thousand Dollars ($125,000). The initial
option payment shall be applicable against
this purchase price, but the extension payment shall not be. The purchase price shall
be paid on exercise of the option, but not
later than on commencement of principal
photography of the motion picture.

In the event one or more motion pictures are released as a theatrical motion
picture in the United States prior to the
initial network broadcast of the pictures,
Producer shall pay Authors a theatrical
release bonus in the amount of One Hundred
Twenty-five Thousand Dollars ($125,000), per
such motion picture.

In the even one or more such motion
pictures are released as a theatrical motion
in the United States subsequent to the initial network broadcast of the motion picture
or is released as a theatrical motion picture in foreign release (with a bona fide
distribution as a theatrical release), or a
television sequel is produced based on the
literary material, Producer shall pay Authors a theatrical releases bonus, or sequel
payment, in the amount of Sixty-two Thousand
Five Hundred Dollars ($62,500).

Authors shall be employed as technical
consultants on each such motion picture for
a total fee in the amount of Fifty Thousand

Dollars ($50,000). Such fee shall be payable as follows: Ten Thousand Dollars ($10,000) shall be payable during the script development phase of the motion picture, subject to the applicable broadcast network agreeing to recognize such fee as a development cost of the motion picture, but in no event later than during production of the motion pictures; and Forty Thousand Dollars ($40,000) shall be payable during production of the motion picture.

In the event that the broadcast network orders an episodic one-hour dramatic prime time series based on the property, Producer will pay Authors a series sales bonus in the amount of Twenty Thousand Dollars ($20,000) based on an order consisting of twelve (12) episodes, which bonus shall be reducible to a floor of Ten Thousand Dollars ($10,000) on a pro-rata basis if the network orders fewer than twelve (12) episodes.

Authors shall be employed as and shall receive on screen and paid advertising credit as technical consultants on the series for a total fee of Seven Thousand Five Hundred dollars ($7,500) per episode for the first season and ten percent (10%) cumulative increases each season thereafter.

Producer shall pay a series royalty in the amount of Two Thousand Five Hundred

Page Three

Dollars ($2,500) per episode during the first broadcast season on the series, which royalty shall increase by Five Hundred Dollars ($500) per episode in the second and subsequent broadcast seasons on the series.

In addition to the foregoing, Producer shall pay Authors two and one half percent of one hundred percent (2.5% of 100%) of the net profits attributable to the exhibition of the motion picture(s) and the series episodes (if applicable). Net profits shall be defined, accounted for and paid in accordance with Producer's standard Definition of Net Profits-Motion Picture - Episodic Series, which definition shall be subject to good faith negotiations on a favored nations basis with any executive producers, script writers, or directors.

Producer will pay Authors advances against the foregoing net profit participation in the amount of Two Thousand Five Hundred Dollars ($2,500) per episode, beginning at the episode number 67 and continuing thereafter, with all such advances retroactive to episode number 1. Advances will be paid at such time as the series is placed into domestic syndication, provided that payment of such advances shall not put Producer in a negative cash flow position, being defined as all actual out-of-pocket production costs (excluding any production

Page Four

fee or overhead charge) plus interest
thereon.

All payments made pursuant to the
terms of this agreement shall be made to the
PMA Literary and Film Management, Inc.,
Federal ID number ##-#######.
If the forgoing is in accordance with your
understanding of our agreement, I will pre-
pare a formal contract.
Sincerely,
Vice President Business Affairs
Producer
Agreed to and accepted:
Peter Miller, President
PMA Literary and Film Management, Inc.

By _____
    Peter Miller

By _____

S.S.# _____
      Ms. Author

By _____

S.S.# _____
      Mr. Author

Page Five

THE NONFICTION BOOK PROPOSAL

ONE

THE ACCIDENTAL MILLIONAIRE

This proposal for an unauthorized biography of Steve Jobs, the man who created Apple Computer, sold to Paragon House Publishers. The book was published in hardcover in 1987; the trade paperback was published in Spring, 1989; Knightsbridge Publishing published the mass-market paperback edition a year after that. The motion picture rights to this book were optioned and the film is in active development.

ACCIDENTAL MILLIONAIRE
The Rise and Fall of Steve Jobs
at Apple Computer
A Proposal for an Unauthorized Biography
Approximately 400 pages
Photos Included

By Lee Butcher

You could hardly imagine two person-
alities that were as disparate as those of
Steve Jobs, co-founder of the Apple Computer
Company, and John C. Sculley. Jobs, who
until the middle of 1985 was Chairman of the
Board and head of the elite Macintosh Division of the Cupertino, California, company,
has been considered by many as the driving
force behind one of the most successful
business enterprises in history. He is
widely believed to have been responsible for
the creation of the first Apple computer,
usually taking the spotlight away from
Stephen Wozniak, the electronics genius who
actually designed and built what was to
become a revolutionary device that spurred
the development of a multi-billion dollar
industry.

There are just as many, and perhaps
more, who think Jobs bullied his way into
Apple and that he was more of a detriment
than an asset. Not long after Apple became
a public company, he had developed a reputation for being willful, dominating, divi-
sive, arrogant, and mercurial. Apple was in
disarray and morale was a shambles when
Sculley became president of the company in
1983 and a large part of it was Jobs' doing.
Less than three years after Sculley joined
Apple, Jobs was stripped of all operating
power and eventually resigned as chairman
after a bitter fight with Sculley and the

Board. Sculley, a traditionalist, was voted
chairman in addition to his duties as president.

Even by Silicon Valley standards,
where the unusual is often the norm, Jobs
was considered quirky. He wore his hair
long, went barefoot, and threw himself with
almost manic obsession into such things as
diets that were supposed to reduce "un-
healthy" mucous from the body, fruitarian
diets that he thought eliminated the need
for bathing, and had a long-lasting flirta-
tion with the mysticism of India. He would
fast for days.

"Whatever Steve did, he became ob-
sessed with it," says one of his acquaintances from the early days before Apple. "He
was a fanatic and it was hard to be around
him because he was constantly lecturing
others."

This facet of Jobs' personality never
changed. A stock analyst who watches Apple
says: "We had hoped that Steve would grow up
with the business, but he never did." He
was driven to be the self-appointed expert
in whatever enterprise he undertook, and to
say that it made him unpopular would be an
understatement. Even Wozniak never really
liked or trusted him. "He will use everyone
to his own advantage," Wozniak says. Jobs'
dominating personality manifested itself at
an early age. When his adoptive parents

were forced to move for economic reasons,
Jobs attended an elementary school he didn't
like. He told his parents that he would not
continue at the school under any circumstances. They gave in to his demands and
moved so Jobs could attend an elementary
school more to his liking.

He defied them shortly after graduation from high school when he announced that
he was going to live with his girlfriend,
Nancy Rogers, in the Santa Cruz mountains
for the summer. His parents replied, "No,
you're not." Jobs retorted, "Yes, I am,"
and walked out the door. Jobs was determined to attend Reed College, an expensive,
ultra-liberal institution in Portland, Oregon, but his father, an engineer at
Hewlett-Packard, argued that his son should
attend a more traditional college. Jobs
informed his parents that if he couldn't go
to Reed, he would not attend any college.
The elder Jobs gave in. Once more the parents submitted to a head-strong son over
whom they had little, if any, control.

The senior Jobs paid thousands of
dollars to support Steve, who soon lost
interest in classes and stopped attending.
Even on a campus noted for the bizarre, Jobs
was considered weird. Before long he
dropped out of classes completely and became
a "floater," moving from one vacant dormi-
tory room to another. His main interest was

in Eastern mysticism and he spent a goodly
portion of his time with the Hare Krishnas
searching for "enlightenment." He had no
idea what he wanted to do with his life.

Wozniak, however, had thrown himself
head over heels into the world of electronics and was immersed in a highly illegal
activity known as "phone phreaking." He had
created a "Blue Box" that allowed him to
make telephone calls around the world without the nuisance of paying for them. He had
met Jobs a few years earlier and the two
teenagers had struck up a guarded friendship. Jobs convinced Wozniak that they
should form a partnership to manufacture and
sell the Blue Boxes to college students.
The illegal venture made the young men edgy
and they dropped it after about a year.

Wozniak turned to the world of micro-
computers, a field still in its infancy. He
was an avid member of the Homebrew Computer
Club in California and took great delight in
showing his latest creations to other computer hobbyists. He did not meet with instant success but, by ingenious use of mi-
crochips, he eventually created a sensation
among his peers. Jobs again saw commercial
possibilities for the circuit board that
Wozniak had designed. He persuaded Wozniak
that they could make money if the circuit
board was refined. They established a garage workshop at Jobs' parents' home.

Wozniak had little interest in fame and
fortune and had to be constantly prodded by
Jobs, who pleaded, begged, and even had
weeping fits to keep Wozniak working.

Wozniak was still a full-time engineer
at Hewlett-Packard and worked on the computer part-time. Jobs scrounged for parts
and became expert at finding them for rock-
bottom prices. The business was called
Apple in remembrance of Jobs' days with the
Hare Krishnas where he picked the fruit in
an orchard. He also scouted for investors
to keep the financially strapped business
from going under. His appearance, abrasive
manner, and lack of experience made it hard.
Apple also needed guidance in marketing and
advertising, but had no money to pay for
professional services.

Jobs was guided by acquaintances at
Intel, a company that manufactures semiconductors, to the Regis McKenna Advertising
and Public Relations Agency. Frank Burgess
had the task of screening potential accounts
and was not enthusiastic, but Jobs launched
an all-out telephone campaign, leaving
stacks of messages, until Burgess decided to
pay Jobs and Wozniak a courtesy call.

His initial misgivings were compounded
when he first met Jobs, who emerged from the
kitchen in sandals, jeans, long unwashed
hair, and a straggly beard. He thought Jobs
was just another Silicon Valley flake until

the unkempt young man started talking. The
full impact of Jobs' personality hit him
like a thunderbolt and he was struck by two
thoughts: first, Jobs was smart, and second,
he was so smart that Burgess didn't know
what in hell Jobs was talking about. Burgess checked further and discovered that the
company had the potential to become a
moneymaker. The agency agreed to handle all
of Apple's marketing for a share of sales
revenue, but hedged its bets by saying that
the results of Apple's first advertisement
should be reviewed before the commitment was
carried further.

Considering the phenomenal success of
other Silicon Valley companies that had
grown from garage enterprises into multi-
million-dollar companies, the McKenna agency
was not taking much of a risk. A memo concerning Apple noted that the company had
experienced little success in selling its
computers to end users, even though it had
moved a quantity to distributors. Wozniak
and Jobs were young and inexperienced, but
the memo compared them to Nolan Bushnell who
was young when he started Atari and was
currently reported to have a net worth of
$10 million.

Apple's plans were far greater than
its financial resources in 1976. The micro-
computer industry as a whole was growing
much faster than Apple. The company needed

money and marketing guidance and Jobs turned
to Bushnell, where he had once worked, for
advice on finding investors. Bushnell educated Jobs about the world of venture capitalists, but warned him, "The longer you can
do without those guys, the better off you
are." The meeting ended with Bushnell giving Jobs the names of three potential investors, one of whom was Don Valentine, who had
invested in Atari during its infancy.

Valentine was a hard-nosed venture
capitalist who was not likely to be bowled
over by a glib teenager like Jobs. He had
started his own venture capital firm, Se-
quoia Ventures, after making a fortune with
other successful investments. He was, in
almost every way, the antithesis of Jobs.
He was a fashionable dresser and was fas-
tidious about his personal appearance, and
equally careful about his investments. He
had met Jobs briefly when the latter worked
at Atari and remarked that Jobs "looked like
a refugee from the human race." (When he
worked at Atari, Jobs was on the fruit diet,
which he believed eliminated the need for
bathing. His co-workers did not agree and
insisted that something had to be done because he smelled so bad they couldn't stand
to be around him. Jobs was eventually
shunted off to a private cubicle.)

Valentine's meeting with Jobs and
Wozniak did not go well. The two young

entrepreneurs were not talking big enough to
suit him. They were satisfied with nibbling
away at the fringes of the single board
computer market, hoping to sell 1,000 units
a year. This was guaranteed to turn Valentine away. "If someone wants to be a millionaire, I'm not interested," he said. "If
he wants a net worth of $50 million to $100
million, I'm interested. If he talks in
terms of billions, I'm interested, because
if he even comes close, we'll both make a
killing." His assessment of Jobs and
Wozniak underlined his lack of enthusiasm
for Apple. "Neither of them knew anything
about marketing or the size of the potential
market," he said. "In short, they weren't
thinking big enough."

Although Valentine declined to invest,
he suggested three venture capitalists whose
interests might mesh with those of Jobs and
Wozniak. One of them was Mike Markkula, a
thirty-three-year-old millionaire but, in
Silicon Valley terms, a "small" millionaire.
Markkula was living a luxurious retirement
when he agreed to meet with Wozniak and
Jobs. His most recent association had been
with Intel. In Silicon Valley, where the
pursuit of worldly pleasures rivals those of
the most exaggerated soap opera, Markkula
was a straight arrow. He preferred home to
life in the fast lane. At Intel, he had
been considered competent and steady, but no

one saw him as a person who was going to
create thunder and lightning. Markkula
borrowed heavily to buy Intel stock and,
when the company went public, he became a
millionaire overnight.

Markkula's meeting with Wozniak and
Jobs marked a major turning point at Apple.
He was impressed with the computer Wozniak
had built and agreed to help organize the
company. After talking it over with his
wife, he agreed to invest $250,000 to de-
velop the Apple II and to devote four years
of his life to the company.

Markkula's tie with Apple had implica-
tions far beyond the money he invested. He
brought a steadying influence, knowledge of
management and marketing, and experience
gained in the rough and tumble world of
business and venture capital. He was a
moderating influence who helped keep Jobs
from running rough-shod over people, a sympathetic audience for Wozniak, who needed
constant assurance and praise, and a vision
for Apple that far exceeded that of either
of the two youngsters. In retrospect, it is
fair to say that there would have been no
Apple Computer Company if it had not been
for Markkula's guiding hand.

Markkula met with Jobs and Wozniak on
weekends and in the evenings to discuss
Apple's future. Arguments arose over the
division of the stock, with Wozniak openly

questioning the importance of Jobs to the
organization. To Wozniak's surprise,
Markkula came to Jobs' defense. "He had a
lot of confidence in Steve," Wozniak said
later. "He saw him as a future executive, a
future Mike Markkula."

Wozniak had little faith in Apple's
future and believed that Markkula would lose
every dime he had invested. He deliberated
over whether to place all of his eggs in one
basket or to accept a transfer to Oregon
with Hewlett-Packard. Both Wozniak and his
first wife liked the security that came with
a regular paycheck. Meanwhile, Markkula and
Jobs were trying to decide whether or not
Apple could continue without Wozniak and
agreed that it could not. They pressured
him into a decision by telling him he had to
join Apple full-time or he was out. Even
then Wozniak dallied. Jobs launched a campaign to convince Wozniak that his future
was with Apple. He telephoned Wozniak's
friends and asked for their help in persuad-
ing him to stay with Apple. As a last re-
sort he visited Wozniak's parents where he
begged for their help. Wozniak's parents
scolded Jobs, telling him that he was an
opportunist who had capitalized on their
son's work and that he deserved no part of
the company. Jobs left the meeting in
tears.

Markkula plotted a more practical approach to entice Wozniak to hitch his star to Apple. He presented a strong argument as to the future prospects for the company and was able to get Wozniak to share his own vision. "He started talking about money, about a computer we could sell, and that decided it for me," Wozniak remembers. "I decided to stay with Apple."

Apple Computer Company was officially formed on January 3, 1977. It bought out the partnership that consisted of Jobs, Wozniak and Markkula for $5,308.96. Markkula's most pressing concern then was to find someone to run the company. A man who came to Markkula's mind was Michael Scott, whose career had been interwoven with his own.

Scott, a native of Gainesville, Florida, had attended the California Institute of Technology where he majored in physics. He had worked at Beckman Instruments Systems Division in Southern California where he helped build equipment to check Saturn rockets before lift-off. He was hired by Fairchild Industries, but quickly became disenchanted with corporate politics, and left for National Semiconductor Co. He was overseeing a $30 million production line by the time he was thirty-two. The discomfort he had experienced with corporate life previously continued to plague him and he was also bored by the lack of glamour and

excitement in manufacturing semiconductors.
He was interested in at least exploring the
possibilities when he heard from Markkula.

Wozniak was ecstatic. He said he
would be glad to have anyone but Jobs manag-
ing production. Jobs, on the other hand,
gave the proposal a cool reception, fearing
the loss of power. Markkula, accustomed to
Jobs by this time, convinced him that a
better-managed company, not power, was at
stake. Jobs balanced the loss of power with
the possible financial gains and agreed to
hire Scott as president. He knew that any
combination of himself, Wozniak, or Markkula
could unseat Scott at any time. Scott was
hired for $20,001 a year, one dollar more
than the triumvirate of Jobs, Wozniak, and
Markkula, and became their titular boss.
Scott's biggest worry was whether or not he
could get along with Jobs. It turned out
that they were anathema to each other.

The arrival of Scott was disastrous
for Jobs, who had been accustomed to doing
whatever he wanted. Jobs found himself
confronted with unyielding authority for the
first time in his life. He bridled. When
Apple began growing, Scott issued numbered
security passes to designate employees.
Because he considered technology to be the
most important part of the new company, he
issued Wozniak pass Number One. Jobs was
beside himself. "Who's Number One?" he

demanded. "I want to be Number One." Told
that Wozniak had that number, Jobs coun-
tered, "Let me be Number Zero. Woz can be
Number One, but I want to be Number Zero."
Another time they fought when Jobs wanted to
sign a batch of purchase orders. "I got
here first," Jobs argued. "I should sign
them." Scott replied that he would sign
them and, if he didn't, he would quit.

The four had little in common except
for an interest in high-technology. Jobs
relished money and power and pushed himself
into Apple because he had nothing better to
do. Wozniak was there because he was the
ultimate hobbyist who liked nothing better
than showing off the machines he created.
Markkula became associated with Apple because he saw it as a way to increase his
personal wealth, and Scott wanted to be
president of a company that would leave an
indelible stamp on high-technology.

The Apple II was introduced at the
First West Coast Computer Fair in the spring
of 1977. It was a lightweight computer with
a new switching system that eliminated the
need for a cumbersome and noisy fan to keep
it cool. Jobs was always behind the scene,
cajoling, pushing, rejecting design and
function until he was at least partly satisfied with the computer.

Shows such as the First West Coast
Computer Fair were of monumental importance

to computer companies. Prospective customers came by the hundreds to see the latest
offerings and a start-up company could become successful immediately if its product
aroused enough attention. Markkula understood the importance of displaying the computer and Apple employees in the best light
possible. He rented a booth and paid to
have it look as smart and elegant as he
could. He ordered Jobs to "spruce up" and
sent him out to buy the first suit he had
ever owned. The display made Apple appear
much more impressive than it actually was,
and it began to receive orders.

Apple had moved out of the Jobs' garage and into a suite in a two-story building on Stevens Creek Boulevard in Cupertino.
A plasterboard wall separated a few desks
from the laboratory and assembling areas.
Scott and Jobs continued to battle. Before
Scott, Jobs had done pretty much as he
wanted and now he found his responsibilities
and power limited. Their arguments continued for years and became known as "The
Scotty Wars."

Amid the turmoil and hand-holding,
Markkula went about the business of formu-
lating marketing plans. He was helped by a
casual acquaintance, John Hall, a group
controller for a Palo Alto pharmaceutical
firm. They planned a three-pronged assault:
to hobbyists, physicians, and home users.

Hall was asked to join the company, but demurred. "I couldn't afford the risk of joining a screwy company like Apple."

Jobs irritated and alienated almost everyone with whom he came into contact. He angered suppliers, many of whom were much larger than Apple, with his arrogant and headstrong attitude. When Apple began hiring employees, Jobs interviewed those who were to fill key positions. He would throw his dirty feet up on a coffee table in front of them and dumbfound them with a merciless inquisition. When interviews were held over lunch, he often embarrassed prospective employees by sending his food back and loudly proclaiming that it was nothing but garbage. One Apple employee described Jobs' treatment of people: "He would blow up over the smallest things. He was very obnoxious to them. We all wondered, 'How can you treat another human being like that?'"

Five months after the Apple II was introduced, the strife-ridden company almost went belly up. Apple was gaining a reputation as a company that could not fill its commitments. As inventory piled up and revenues dropped, Apple's thin cushion of cash began to evaporate. Scott and Markkula agreed to underwrite a loan of $250,000 to help keep the company afloat. The tension between Jobs and Scott continued to mount and had a demoralizing effect on the

company's employees. On Jobs' twenty-third
birthday, Scott sent him a funeral wreath
decorated with white roses and bearing the
inscription: "R.I.P. Thinking of you."

The enhanced Apple II used a disk
drive rather than a tape cassette to record
information. It was a triumph of technology. When it was introduced at the Consumer
Electronics Show in 1978, it was an instant
hit. One engineer who saw it says, "I almost dropped my pants. It was so clever."
Apple's orders began to pile up.

Markkula knew that Apple needed reputable investors, not only for cash, but to
lend it a respectable sheen. He was looking
toward the day when Apple would become a
public company and well-known investors
would make Apple much more attractive. He
found the investors he wanted and when the
papers were signed and stock exchanged in
January 1978, Apple was valued at $3 mil-
lion. The company was starting to receive
serious attention on Wall Street and in the
nation's business press.

By September 1980, three and a half
years after the Apple II was introduced,
revenues rose from $7.8 million to $117.9
million and profits increased from $793,497
to $11.7 million. There were more than
1,000 on Apple's payroll. But for all of
its seeming success, the core of Apple was
rotting with internal strife. Not only did

Jobs constantly harass, humiliate, and berate employees, but Scott's personality seemed to change overnight and he began doing the same thing, possibly because he was in pain from a serious eye infection that doctors feared might cause permanent blindness. The company touted itself as one having high humanistic ideals, but, in practice, it had become a stressful, difficult place to work. Scott issued terse memos and became a heavy-handed disciplinarian. The appearance of either Jobs or Scott at an employee's desk could cause a constriction in the throat and clenching of the stomach muscles. As the lesser of two evils, Scott was fired, a move that threw him into a deep depression. The drapes and curtains at his house remained closed for weeks as he struggled to come to terms with his personal and professional disaster.

There was no one to replace Scott as president except Markkula. Jobs was too young, inexperienced, and mercurial to be trusted to do the job. Markkula, whose four years he had pledged to Apple were drawing to a close, reluctantly became president while Jobs replaced him as Chairman of the Board. Jobs, meanwhile, was having his own personal problems. Nancy Rogers, his boyhood sweetheart with whom he had lived, filed a paternity suit against him. Jobs steadfastly denied that he was the father

and refused to pay the $20,000 settlement
Rogers sought. Markkula didn't think that
was enough and urged Jobs to settle for
$80,000. He refused. To the surprise of
everyone who knew him, he agreed to a blood
test to determine paternity. The results
stated that it was 94.4 percent positive
that Jobs was the father of Rogers' daughter, Lisa. Jobs chose to look at it another
way: "All it shows is that 15.4 percent of
all the men in America could be the father."
He finally agreed to pay $385 a month in
child support and to settle $5,856 in public
assistance that Rogers had received.

In spite of the turmoil, Apple was
thriving. In 1977, the partnership of Jobs,
Wozniak, and Apple had been valued at
$5,308. On New Year's Day in 1980, three
weeks after Apple went public, the company
was valued at $1.788 billion, which was more
than Ford Motor Company and four times
Lockheed. The public stock offering was one
of the most sensational in history and, in
the hyperbolic parlance of Silicon Valley,
created instant "zillionaires." Jobs'
shares were valued at $256.4 million.

As Chairman and operating head of the
Macintosh division, Jobs created deep and
bitter resentments and rivalries, pitting
department against department, division
against division. Jobs had more of a pen-
chant for losing friends than for making

them. One of the first casualties was
Wozniak, who had left Apple totally disillu-
sioned, not only with Jobs but with the
corporation Apple had become. He is still
bitter. "Even in personal conversations
with the guy, you could never really tell
what he was thinking," Wozniak says. "Ask
him a 'yes' or 'no' question and the answer
said 'no' to anyone who heard it, but the
answer was 'maybe yes, maybe no.' He puts
his own interests ahead of anyone else.
Aside from not being able to trust him, he
will use anyone to his own advantage."

Apple was being severely hurt by other
computer companies and Jobs' unwillingness
to conform to the marketplace. Jobs insisted that the end users take what Apple
offered and do the conforming. He had also
seriously underestimated the entry of IBM
into the personal computer market. In fact,
when IBM announced that intention, he published an advertisement that read, "Welcome
IBM. Seriously." Apple failed to deliver
computers on time, further increasing its
reputation as a company that could not meet
commitments. Jobs dallied, procrastinated,
and rejected design after design of an
enhanced Macintosh computer to the point
that its designers were discouraged and
placed little importance on timetables.
"It didn't matter when you got it in," one
engineer said. "You knew he was going
to reject it anyhow."

IBM was able to bite deeply into the personal computer market with a philosophy that was diametrically opposed to that of Jobs. Instead of building a computer to its own expectations, it sent hundreds of representatives into the field to determine what customers wanted, then incorporated those features into its designs. In 1980, Apple had 32 percent of the personal computer market for those in the $1,000 to $5,000 price range. By 1985, Apple's market share had dropped to 24 percent even though the market was blossoming.

Not long after Apple's stock offering, the Board of Directors began looking for a strong president to replace Markkula, who longed to return to his interrupted retirement, millions wealthier than he had been previously. The man who caught the Board's attention was John C. Sculley, President of the Pepsi-Cola division of PepsiCo. Sculley was credited with breaking Coca-Cola's monopoly at soda fountains across the nation and for developing a market campaign that allowed Pepsi to bite deeply into Coke's market.

Sculley's background was traditional. He had graduated with a degree in architecture, but abandoned that interest in favor of an MBA from the University of Pennsylvania's Wharton School of Business. When Sculley joined PepsiCo in 1967, he was

sent straight to the shipping docks to learn
the business from the ground up. Although
he didn't have to, he spent long hours load-
ing heavy cartons of soft drinks on delivery
trucks. He even worked out with weights
each night at the YMCA to become stronger so
his job performance would improve. "That
wasn't required of the job, but he wanted to
make good," says Charles V. Mangold, a
PepsiCo senior vice president who was
Sculley's supervisor at the time. "He
wanted a total background." Sculley was
married to the daughter of PepsiCo's chairman when he joined the company, but his
worth was proven when he was retained after
the marriage broke up. Sculley and his
former wife's father remained fast friends
as well as business associates.

When Apple turned its attention to
him, Sculley was a member of the PepsiCo
Board of Directors, Keep America Beautiful,
and the Soft Drink Association. He also
lectured weekly at Wharton. He was considered somewhat of a cold fish with strong
ideas about marketing and traditional business management. He was as different from
Jobs as night is from day. Sculley had a
passing interest in technology but was a
babe in the woods when it came to the intri-
cate workings of computers.

Individual Board members at Apple
wooed Sculley privately, then Jobs was given

the task of recruiting him. Sculley had
misgivings about joining Apple, largely
because he was concerned about whether or
not he could get along with Jobs, whose
reputation had spread far beyond the confines of Silicon Valley. The two men spent
hours together chatting, walking through
leafy parks on both the East and West Coast.
They didn't talk about business or computers, but about poetry, art, and Eastern
philosophy. Later, Apple's public relations
machine said they got along famously and the
company line was, "They were like brothers,
or sometimes like father and son. [Sculley
was fifteen years older than Jobs.] They
would finish each other's sentences." In
retrospect, it appears that the two men may
have been more like gladiators circling one
another, looking for strengths and weak-
nesses. Sculley had also been assured privately of the Board's support. Apple offered Sculley a sweet deal. He was guaranteed salary and bonuses of $2 million for
his first year and help in buying a $2 mil-
lion home.

Sculley joined Apple in 1983 as President and so began a bloodbath of frightening
proportions. Sculley, who had pledged to
operate Apple in non-traditional ways, went
about his job in a distinctly traditional
manner. He immediately consolidated five
divisions into two and took charge of one

division himself to improve sagging company
morale. Within a year he had fired more
than 1,000 Apple employees and only eight
senior executives remained of the fourteen
who were there when he was hired. Sculley's
arrival in 1983 heralded a banner year for
Apple, with stock rising from $22 to $62 per
share, increasing Jobs' holdings in the
company to $432 million. The Macintosh,
long delayed, was finally launched in 1984,
selling a record of 70,000 units in just one
hundred days.

Jobs had finally succeeded in turning
the Board against him. Sculley was told
that he must get the Macintosh division,
which Jobs headed, in line. He replied,
"It's a little hard to do when the division
head happens to be Chairman of the Board."
When Jobs heard about this, he began his own
campaign to have Sculley fired, but the
Board turned a deaf ear. Jobs' arrogance
and mismanagement had finally caught up with
him and his career at Apple was unraveling.
In May 1985, Jobs was stripped of all opera-
tional authority even though he remained
Chairman of the Board. The full impact did
not hit Jobs until later when he found himself isolated within the company and important company papers bypassed his desk. No
one bothered to return his telephone calls.
The Apple public relations machine, seeking
to minimize controversy, issued a statement

saying that Jobs would remain as "the soul
of Apple." But Jobs knew that he had been
castrated.

He resigned September 17, 1985, and
told Sculley that he was taking a few employees with him to start a company he
called "NeXT". He showed Sculley a list of
names and vows that Sculley raised no objec-
tion. Sculley remembers it differently.
"He was taking key people who knew Apple's
secrets. The Board was alarmed." Apple
filed suit against its former Chairman and
co-founder but eventually settled out of
court. In the middle of 1986, as a last
gesture of defiance, Jobs sold all of his
shares in Apple except one.

In less than a decade, Apple had risen
from a corner garage business to a multi-
national company worth $2 billion. The
contribution that Jobs made cannot be overlooked, but it has often been exaggerated in
the nation's press. He was the visionary
who saw a business in Wozniak's ventures as
a computer hobbyist and it was he who
scrounged for parts and saw the need for
outside investors. It is accurate to say
that, without Jobs, there would have been no
Apple Computer. He is the one who brought
Markkula, with his cash and vision, on
board, and who kept Wozniak working when the
latter showed little faith.
Jobs was only thirty years old when he was

ousted as Chairman of Apple. Nick Arnett, high-technology reporter for the <u>San Jose Business Journal</u>, said: "Without Jobs, Apple is just another company. And without Apple, Steve Jobs is just another Silicon Valley millionaire."

OUTLINE

1. Introduction. Jobs in the final days of
his career with Apple. He has achieved great
wealth and power as co-founder of Apple and
Chairman of the Board. Now he sits isolated
in his office knowing that he has been
usurped by John Sculley. It was not always
that way.

2. The Rebel. Jobs was a loner as a youth
and not at all popular with his peers. He
also was able to dominate his adoptive parents. He was interested in high-technology
and attended evening classes offered by
Hewlett-Packard. He attends Reed College
and drops out for lack of interest and
throws himself into Eastern philosophy,
practicing various diets and fasting. He
spends time with Hare Krishnas searching for
enlightenment. Later he spends time bumming
around India, gets scabies, and leaves the
country in despair, vowing that Thomas
Edison had done more to improve the world
than all religious philosophies put together.

3. Jobs meets Stephen Wozniak who is an avid
"phone phreak." Wozniak has created a "Blue
Box" that allows him to make telephone calls
around the world without paying for them.
Jobs persuades Wozniak to enter into a part-

nership to make and sell Blue Boxes to college students, a moderately successful, but
illegal venture with risks that soon force
them to shut down. The two men have little
in common except that they are both interested in high-technology and are loners with
few friends.

4. The Homebrew Computer Club. Wozniak and
Jobs are both members of this club, which is
composed of avid computer hobbyists.
Wozniak works on various computer boards and
eventually creates a sensation with a single
circuit board. Jobs sees commercial possibilities and they establish a workshop in
Jobs' garage to manufacture and sell the
boards. Jobs has to prod Wozniak to improve
the board while he scrounges for parts and
looks for investors. He is eventually
steered to Mike Markkula, a "small" Silicon
Valley millionaire who has retired at age
thirty-three.

5. Markkula becomes fascinated with Apple
and decides to invest $250,000 of his own
money to develop the Apple II computer and
to devote four years of his life to organize
the company. Wozniak has little faith in
the venture and predicts that Markkula will
lose every penny of his investment. He
considers leaving Apple and accepting a
transfer to Oregon with Hewlett-Packard,

where he works as an engineer. He decides
to stay with Apple after an intense campaign
by Jobs and Markkula to keep him. Apple
Computer Company is formed and buys out the
partnership for under $6000.

6. Markkula begins to organize Apple. He
hires Scott to become President of the company. Wozniak is ecstatic because he would
prefer anybody heading operations rather
than Jobs. Jobs bridles at Scott's arrival
because his power is limited now. For the
first time in his life he meets with unyielding authority. Scott and Jobs dislike
each other from the beginning and a long-
running battle between the two eventually
becomes known as "The Scotty Wars."

7. Apple begins to have success with the
introduction of the enhanced Apple II at the
First West Coast Computer Fair. Markkula,
through an impressive display booth, makes
Apple appear to be a more substantial company than it really is. He orders Jobs to
spruce up and sends him out to buy his first
suit. The Fair results in a number of orders for Apple and the company moves from
the garage into a suite in Cupertino. Jobs
and Scott continue feuding as the company
starts to grow. Jobs displays an arrogant
attitude toward suppliers and employees and
divisiveness and confusion is apparent

within the company. Apple gains a reputation as a company that can't fulfill its
commitments and almost goes belly up.
Markkula and Scott underwrite a $250,000
loan to keep the company afloat.

8. Markkula goes about the business of preparing a business plan as internal strife
continues. He knows that the company must
have well-known and respected investors to
give it cash and credentials. He is already
looking forward to the day when Apple will
become a public company. Markkula finds the
investors he wants and Apple starts to receive attention on Wall Street and in the
nation's business press.

9. As Apple becomes more successful, the
internal strife intensifies. Scott suffers
from an eye infection that doctors fear may
cause permanent blindness. He becomes dictatorial and, added to the problems that
Jobs causes, there is terror in the ranks of
Apple employees. The turmoil causes computers to be shipped too quickly to distributors, often without manuals on how to operate them. There is little software being
developed for the Apple computers. Apple's
executive board fires Scott, and Markkula
reluctantly steps in as president while Jobs
becomes Chairman of the Board.

10. Apple goes public in one of the most
spectacularly successful stock offerings in
history. Jobs' shares are worth $256.4
million. Apple is now worth $1.788 billion,
which is more than Ford Motor Company and
four times the value of Lockheed. Jobs, in
the meantime, is hit with a paternity suit
from his boyhood sweetheart and live-in
companion. She is willing to settle for
$20,000 but Jobs disclaims his responsibil-
ity, even though Markkula urges him to pay
$80,000 to settle the case. Jobs takes a
blood test to determine paternity and results show it is almost certain that he is
the father. He is forced to pay $385 a
month in child support payments and to
settle public assistance debts for the
child.

11. Apple has trouble meeting its commitments because of divisiveness within its
ranks. Jobs, who is head of the Macintosh
division, creates an elite corps that in-
creases the internal strife. He does not
abide by company policies even though he
expects others to follow them to the letter.
The Macintosh is not completed, as promised,
because Jobs rejects design after design.
Engineers and technicians in the division
pay little attention to timetables because
they are convinced Jobs will reject anything
they propose.

12. Markkula is anxious to return to his interrupted retirement. The Apple Board privately woos John C. Sculley, a strong marketer and manager who is president of Pepsi Cola. Sculley's major concern is whether or not he can get along with Jobs, whose reputation for arrogance has spread far beyond the confines of Silicon Valley. The two men meet several times and discuss art, poetry, and philosophy. Sculley, assured privately of the Board's support, and offered $2 million a year in salary and bonuses, plus help in buying a $2 million home, joins Apple as president. The Apple public relations machine pumps out the official line that Sculley and Jobs get along like soulmates.

13. Sculley's arrival starts a bloodbath. He had pledged to operate Apple in non-traditional ways, but he goes about his job in a distinctly traditional manner. He consolidates divisions and fires 1,000 employees. A year after his arrival only eight of the fourteen senior executives who were with Apple remain. Sculley's arrival also heralds a banner year for Apple with stock almost tripling in value and the Macintosh finally ready to market. More than 70,000 units are sold in the first month.

14. The Board has finally wearied of the
turmoil that Jobs causes and his mismanagement of the Macintosh division. Sculley is
ordered to shape up the division. He re-
plies that it is hard to do so when the
division head is Chairman of the Board.
Jobs hears about this and launches a campaign to have Sculley fired, but the Board
turns a deaf ear. Jobs is stripped of all
operating authority, even though the company
says he will remain as "the soul" of Apple
and retain his position as Chairman. Jobs
finds himself in exile within the company.
He has been thoroughly castrated.

15. Jobs resigns as Chairman to start a new
company he calls "NeXT". He shows Sculley a
list of people he wants to take with him
from Apple and says that Sculley raised no
objections. Sculley recalls the incident
differently and says that Jobs would denude
Apple by taking key employees. Apple files
a suit against its co-founder and former
Chairman but eventually settles. Jobs, in a
final gesture of defiance, sells all of his
Apple stock except one share.

16. Epilogue. Jobs played an important part
at Apple in its early days by seeing opportunities for the circuit board Wozniak created. Even though he went about it in an
abrasive way, he was the one who found parts

for Wozniak at prices they could afford, and who brought Markkula on board. There probably would have been no Apple Computer Company without him. At thirty he was worth nearly $500 million and may have reached the pinnacle of his career. It will be hard for him to top his achievement at Apple, even though he is confident that he can, through a blending of computers with education. A business writer in Silicon Valley noted, "Without Jobs, Apple is just another company. Without Apple, Steve Jobs is just another Silicon Valley millionaire."

THE MARKET — Steve Jobs is one of the most fascinating entrepreneurs in the history of American business. He is brusque, abrasive, ingenious, mesmerizing, an enigma of driving ambition coupled with a life-long devotion to the gentle philosophies of the East. Jobs has been the "whiz kid" of America's personal computer industry and has been publicized on the covers of major national magazines, television spots, newspapers, and is the subject of endless fascination. His fight with John Sculley at Apple, which resulted in his being kicked out of the company he helped form, has brought Jobs even more prominently into the limelight. His story is one of controversy: a hippie who became a "zillionaire" when he was twenty-one; a ruthless businessman who has

the heart of a poet-philosopher. This is a
type of story that has aroused interest
around the world in the past. Jobs already
has the status of folk hero and is a star in
the world of big business; the national
publicity concerning his battle with
Sculley, and his shocking defeat, make him
an ideal subject for a biographical book.

THE AUTHOR — Lee Butcher is a veteran writer
and journalist who was editor of the <u>San
Jose Business Journal</u> in Silicon Valley when
the rift developed between Jobs and John
Sculley. He was the first to report the
conflict to the public. Butcher is intimately familiar with Silicon Valley, Apple,
and has contacts in Silicon Valley who have
promised to talk with him, either for or not
for attribution. Butcher is the author of
four nonfiction books and the author or co-
author of four novels. He has written for
<u>Forbes</u>, <u>Business Week</u>, <u>Barron's</u>, and other
national business and general interest maga-
zines, and has been the editor of <u>Texas
Business</u> and <u>Florida Trend</u>, the nation's two
leading regional business magazines.

TWO

FATAL FREEWAY

The following is a proposal for a true-crime book called *Fatal Freeway*, by Steve Salerno. My company successfully placed the book based on this proposal during a literary auction we conducted. Clarkson N. Potter, a division of Random House, Inc., outbid several other publishers for the hardcover rights. The television movie rights were optioned, but they lapsed; we are working on developing this as a movie of the week for network or cable television.

FATAL FREEWAY
A True Crime Proposal

By Steve Salerno

Twenty-year-old Cara Knott was the
kind of daughter mothers dream about. She
was lovely to look at — physically at least,
the classic California blonde. But Cara was
also bright and articulate, unerringly po-
lite, socially aware, a devoted church-goer
who performed volunteer work for several
causes around the quiet San Diego suburb in
which she lived. In the libertine atmosphere of San Diego State University (ranked
by Playboy magazine as one of the nation's
top ten party schools), Cara had nonetheless
established herself as a girl who subscribed
to life's traditional values. She had one
boyfriend whom she planned to marry in a few
years, once both of them were more established. She did not believe in "playing the
field." And yet, Cara was not preachy. She
was, as a close college friend put it,
"someone who always finds the common denomi-
nator. With Cara, everybody feels at ease."

Cara's feeling for humanity did not
cloud her awareness of the dangers of modern
living. Though celebrated for her numerous
acts of good Samaritanship, the recent
graduate of a police course on self-defense
for women knew how to avoid potentially
dangerous situations. Her credo being "Better safe than sorry," she was appalled at
some of the unnecessary risks her more
devil-may-care friends would take during
their late-night escapades.

Later, those friends would talk about
the irony of tragedy's having chosen Cara
Knott for a victim.

On December 27, 1986, Cara drove to
the North County home of her boyfriend,
Wayne Bautista, for an uncharacteristic
Friday night visit. Wayne hadn't been feeling well, and they had been unable to spend
much time together over Christmas. Although
their schedules were such that they ordi-
narily saw each other only on Saturdays or
Sundays, Cara thought a special pre-weekend
stopover might be therapeutic.

After spending an hour or so with
Wayne, she left his house at about 8:45. As
was her custom, she had phoned her parents
just before leaving to tell them she was on
her way. Cara then pulled into a gas station near a major shopping mall and filled
the tank of her white 1968 Volkswagen
Beetle. She pumped the gas herself, ex-
changing a few Yuletide pleasantries with
the clerk. He would remember her vivacious
manner and her pretty smile.

Several hours later, Cara had still
not arrived home, and the uneasiness Joyce
and Samuel Knott had unaccountably felt all
evening blossomed into full-scale alarm.
Their daughter was not the kind of girl to
make capricious side-trips. If she called
and said she was en route, it meant she was
en route. But Cara was long overdue; the

trip should have taken twenty-five minutes, a half hour at the outside. No more than that.

At 11 p.m., the Knotts attempted to file a missing person claim but were re-buffed by the San Diego Sheriff's Office. Their daughter had simply not been gone long enough, they were told. An hour later, frustrated with sitting and waiting, the Knotts decided to recruit a search party from among neighbors and nearby relatives. So well-liked was Cara that they had no trouble doing so, despite the lateness of the hour. By 12:30, the ad hoc posse had deployed itself at intervals along the main north-south freeway in an effort to find the girl.

Not until the following morning did their search bear fruit. At 8:30 a.m. Cara's brother-in-law, Bill Weick, spotted her abandoned Volkswagen on an obsolete freeway access road, just off the freeway about midway between Wayne's house and the Knott home. The car looked none the worse for wear. The driver's window was down, and Cara's keys remained in the ignition; Weick turned them and the engine promptly started. Recognizing foul play as a distinct likeli-hood, the terrified Knotts once again phoned the police.

This time, the response was swift. And the subsequent news, for Joyce and Samuel Knott, was crushing.

A quarter-mile south of the empty
Volkswagen, the police found Cara Knott's
battered body. She had been strangled and
then tossed seventy-five feet from an old
bridge to the murky ravine below. There
were signs of sexual assault.

Besides sparking a panic among the
residents of the quiet neighborhood in which
the body was found, Cara Knott's killing
mystified investigators. They could not
reconcile the apparent circumstances of her
murder with the few facts that they had to
go on. She had been seen leaving the Chev-
ron station, alone in her car, at about 9
p.m. From there she would have had to drive
just a few hundred feet before entering the
freeway, followed by a straight run of
twenty miles to her home. How had her as-
sailant intercepted her and gained access to
her car? Her father assured everyone she
wasn't the type of person to knowingly place
herself at peril. Pick up a hitchhiker?
Cara? To Sam Knott, it was unthinkable.

An investigator summed up the mood at
police headquarters: "Right now, we're at a
total loss to explain exactly what might
have happened out there on the freeway."

Meantime, in quiet and futile acknowledgment of its role in the Knott case, the
exit ramp that had taken the girl to her
death was hurriedly sealed off. The stretch
of road beneath — called, ironically enough,

Mercy Road — led nowhere anyway; the highway to which it had once given access had itself long since been closed, and therefore, in the words of a sheepish transportation department spokesman, it presented "too much potential danger for the unwary motorist." The action was seen as a clear admission of official negligence, and was expected by some to inspire an immediate lawsuit by Cara's parents. For the time being, however, Sam Knott could only be philosophical.

"It always seems to take a tragedy like this to make people see the things they've overlooked," he said. "We think we've taken all the precautions, and yet we don't realize just how many hidden pitfalls our children face out there." Eventually, Cara's family filed a wrongful death suit for $20 million.

* * *

Officer Craig Alan Peyer was a cop's cop. As 1976 drew to a close, Peyer was completing his thirteenth year with the California Highway Patrol, one of the nation's truly venerated law enforcement agencies (owing at least in part to its depiction in such blockbuster TV series as Highway Patrol and CHiPs). His career with CHP, following a meritorious stint with the Air Force, had been a model of professional dedication and achievement. On several occasions he had been decorated for service above and beyond the call.

At the same time, Peyer was anything
but a gung-ho, Clint Eastwood type. He had
built a reputation for being low key and
helpful, constructively critical rather than
harsh in his treatment of errant motorists.
Craig Peyer was just not the type to harass
drivers "for the hell of it." He even
lacked the hard-bitten look of the career
cop. Peyer's soft, boyish face was a perfect complement to his bedside manner. In
fact, since his earliest days with the force
his colleagues had joked that Peyer should
charge the department a fee for his public
relations services on its behalf.

So it was not surprising that, a year
or so before the Cara Knott case, in the
midst of a series of stop-and-go robberies
of stranded motorists, Peyer had been called
upon by the media to give fearful viewers a
primer on how to protect themselves in such
situations. Public response was so enthusiastic that KGTV, the local ABC affiliate,
has showcased his advice a number of times
since. Peyer seemed to welcome the opportunities to share his professional wisdom and
concern.

On the evening following Cara Knott's
murder, KGTV turned once again to Peyer, who
had himself been on duty the night of Cara
Knott's disappearance. They wanted him to
reassure female drivers, to offer some coun-
termeasures against freeway desperados. As
always, Peyer obliged.

Watching Peyer's performance from their respective homes, some of his fellow officers began to lean a bit closer to the TV screen; they were disturbed by what they thought they saw. On his right cheek was a series of small marks. Not shaving cuts, but the kinds of parallel scratches that might have been caused by a hand being raked across his face: a hand with fairly long nails, the length a young woman would wear them. None of Peyer's CHP buddies recalled seeing such marks on his face when he left to go out on his December 27 shift. Nor had Peyer reported a confrontation or anything else out of the ordinary — though come to think of it, he had seemed rather ill-at-ease during his routine call-ins later that night. And now, on the screen, he struck them as being uncharacteristically agitated. This was not the same laid-back guy they had come to know.

The officers began phoning each other. One of them, who had shared a ride with Peyer a few days earlier, recounted an eerie coincidence. As the two of them were driving past the Mercy Road exit, Peyer had gestured toward the bridge in the background and said, "If you ever wanted to dump a body, that would be the ideal place to do it." At the time, Peyer's companion had attached no special significance to the remark. Now he was troubled.

To Craig Peyer's coworkers, the irony
was excruciating. "Stay in the vehicle, and
lock all doors," they had just heard Peyer
tell his viewing audience. "Even if you
have to wait all night, it's better to be in
the safety of your vehicle than to try to
walk and get assistance. <u>Anything can hap-
pen</u>. Being a female, you can be raped,
robbed, all the way to where you could be
killed. Once you get in that other person's
car, <u>you're at their mercy</u> . . ."

Was it really possible that their
spokesperson and friend, Craig Alan Peyer,
had something to do with Cara Knott's death?

Investigators began a piece-by-piece
reconstruction of Peyer's activities on the
night of the murder. They interviewed a
young San Diego resident named Jean-Pierre
Gulli. Gulli told them he had been driving
on Interstate 15 on the evening of December
27 when he was pulled over by a CHP officer
and cited for having an inoperative tail-
light. Gulli would remember the time as
9:45, "possibly later but definitely no
earlier." His recollection was strong because he had planned to be someplace by ten,
had gotten a late start to begin with, and
was annoyed that the ticket would put him
still further behind schedule. Gulli would
also recall that the officer acted "wired,"
and spent an inordinate amount of time in
his patrol car before returning with the
ticket.

Casually examining the citation as any motorist might, Gulli noticed that an alteration had been made. In the box that said, "time of issuance," the officer had at first written the correct time, 10:20 p.m. Then, for some reason, he had thought better of it, crossed out the original numerals and written over it, 9:20.

Looking down, Gulli had read the signature at the bottom of the ticket as that of one "Craig Peyer, CHP."

Over the next few days, the forensics people worked nonstop. They refined their original account of the murder, determining that Cara had probably been strangled with a heavy rope — carried as standard equipment in the trunks of CHP vehicles — and tossed from the bridge while still alive. (Thus, for Cara's family, there was the thought of the incomprehensible horror those last moments must have held for the daughter they so cherished.) Her time of death was fixed at between 9:00 and 9:30 p.m. Fibers found at the scene were compared with those taken from a rough spot on the pocket of a uniform shirt that was surreptitiously removed from Peyer's locker; there was a disturbing similarity. Tire tread analyses seemed to reveal that a CHP car had been adjacent to Knott's on the lonely exit ramp. Blood that matched Peyer's type was found on Cara's shoes and fingernails.

On January 9, Peyer himself was called
in for questioning, which he at first considered routine. But the length of the
session — some eight hours — and the tone of
the investigator's queries left little doubt
about what was really happening.

Returning home, he sat his wife down
and voiced a shattering prediction.
"They're going to arrest me, Karen," he told
her. "Maybe not tomorrow or next week, but
they're going to arrest me sooner or later
for the murder of Cara Knott." Both of them
began to cry.

On January 15, Peyer's prophecy was
fulfilled. A police caravan roared through
the somnolent tree-lined neighborhood in
which Peyer and his family lived (no more
than five minutes from the site where Cara's
body was found). Two of the cars careened
into Peyer's driveway, and a virtual strike
force of city police and CHP officers hand-
cuffed Peyer in front of his heartsick wife
and frightened children. The Gulli ticket
had been the clincher. Interpreted as an
attempt to fabricate an alibi — one that
would have placed Peyer several miles away
at the time Cara Knott died
— the ticket had led investigators to the
nightmarish conclusion that the killer was,
indeed, one of their own.

In the aftermath of Peyer's arrest,
stunned friends and neighbors rallied to the

officer's defense. Their support went far beyond the usual platitudes about how quiet and friendly the accused was. Convinced, as one neighbor put it, that "time will vindicate Craig Peyer," many of them mortgaged their homes in a successful grassroots campaign to raise Peyer's unprecedented seven-figure bail.

Eventually, Karen Peyer, who with her three children had retreated behind drawn curtains after the arrest, came forward to make a statement about her husband. Briefly she recalled for reporters the circumstances of their courtship and marriage. Less than two years before Craig had been the boy-next-door when Karen's first marriage collapsed. (Peyer's second marriage had gone sour just a year before that.) She praised her embattled husband for his compassion, said that "without his no-strings support and sincerity" she would have been unable to get through that most trying period in her life. "Craig Peyer is the most loving, affectionate, and concerned human being I've ever known," she declared tearfully. "Then one day, someone comes along and says he killed a girl. I say someone is playing a terribly cruel joke on us..."

Still, there must have been doubts. Karen and Craig had been married only a short time, less than eighteen months. In the six years before that, Craig Peyer had gone through two previous marriages.

Despite her steadfast public alle-
giance to her husband, Karen Peyer must have
asked herself, <u>Is there a side to this man I
know nothing about</u>?

* * *

The arrest of a California Highway
Patrolman in the Knott case did little to
quell the anxiety that had plagued San Diego
since the night of the killing. In fact,
the city was gripped by a new, and in many
ways, more chilling kind of fear. The "man
in blue" had become an object of suspicion;
CHP's 4,700 traffic officers suddenly found
themselves operating under a cloud of dis-
honor. As one young woman told a reporter
for the <u>San Diego Union</u>, "It's like being
afraid to go to confession because you think
the priest might try to rape you!" Women
brazenly announced their intentions to ig-
nore police instructions to "pull over."
Still others hinted at the possibility of
arming themselves in the hopes of getting
the drop on any late-night CHP assassins.
Ad hoc counseling centers had to be set up
to help stymied officers deal with the pros-
pect of public intransigence, hostility — or
worse.

CHP Chief Ben Killingsworth tried to
defuse the tensions: "We don't believe there
is any reason for anyone to have any fear
during any subsequent contact with any law

enforcement agency because of this."
Killingsworth stressed the unique and isolated nature of the occurrence. He reminded
everyone that, given the thousands of officers on patrol and the millions of cases
of public contact, the CHP record was nothing if not admirable.

The public was unappeased. For one
thing, as recently as 1982, there had been a
similar unpleasantness. A CHP officer
cruising the deserted stretch of road between California and Las Vegas had raped and
then killed a vacationing Utah woman. And
in 1984, there had been a shooting allegedly
precipitated by racial epithets from the
mouth of a drunken CHP officer. Was there a
laxity in CHP screening procedures? Was
there a weakness in the system that prevented the authorities from predicting when
an officer was about to "snap," as Craig
Peyer seemingly had in the pre-Christmas
weeks of 1986? Newspaper editorialists
pondered the question.

Present, too, was a certain fatalism,
a cynical outlook on the system and one's
chances in the world. San Diego Chief of
Police Bill Kolender understood. "We know
what they're thinking," he sighed during a
televised press conference. "Right now
they're saying, 'Is there anyone left I can
trust?'"

As the investigation proceeded, a subplot as bizarre as the murder itself began to emerge.

Over the past six or eight weeks, Craig Peyer had shown an affinity for pulling over young blond women driving Volkswagen Beetles. The pattern seldom varied: citing some trumped-up charge, he would make the stop, force his quarry to leave the freeway at a deserted exit ramp, and proceed to engage the women in odd conversations that bore little ostensible relevance to the matter at hand. In one case, he had effectively imprisoned a young lady in his squad car for nearly two hours; only when another motorist pulled over to ask directions did Peyer's captive take the opportunity to return to her car and drive off.

Then, on Christmas Eve — just three days before Cara's death — Peyer had behaved strangely in the process of making a stop on a girl who bore a remarkable resemblance to Cara Knott. He had pulled up behind her, flashing his lights, but when she started to pull off onto the freeway shoulder, he ordered her to continue down the off-ramp to the same deserted stretch of road where Cara Knott's car would be found four days later. Without issuing a ticket, Peyer let the woman go after about fifteen minutes, during which time "he acted really, really

friendly, almost flaky," according to the
woman. "He just didn't conduct himself like
a cop. I started getting chills."

Incredibly, prior to Cara Knott's
murder, only one woman thought Peyer's be-
havior sufficiently disquieting to warrant
filing a formal complaint (which suggests
that many of the women were perhaps less
disturbed by his attentions then they would
now like CHP to believe). In that instance,
a man named Sigurd Ziglar wrote a letter to
CHP on behalf of his wife, Donna. He explained that on December 13, Peyer had
pulled over the Ziglar's late-model
Volkswagen "evidently in the belief that
Donna was alone in the car." Ziglar drew
this inference because when Peyer came to
the window and Ziglar, who had been sleeping
in the passenger seat, suddenly roused,
Peyer seemed taken aback. "The officer
offered no legitimate explanation for the
stop, and essentially told us to go on about
our business," wrote Ziglar. "He seemed
flustered. It left us wondering what might
have happened if my wife had actually been
alone in the car." Ziglar's complaint received no formal reply from CHP.

But the most damning piece of circumstantial evidence was to emerge from police
archives in mid-February. Six years before,
on December 28, another blond college coed,
Amy Leibling, had disappeared during one of

Peyer's evening shifts. No connection was
made to the CHP officer at the time, but one
fact stood out now that seemed to link the
unsolved Leibling disappearance to the
present matter.

Like Cara Knott, Amy Leibling had been
driving an older model Volkswagen bug.

The question was tantalizing: Was
Craig Alan Peyer the "Christmas-week killer-
cop"?

                    * * *

Through his attorney, the colorful,
locally celebrated Robert Grimes, Craig
Peyer had been adamant about his innocence.
(Grimes, master of sarcasm and understatement, promises to add a certain comic relief
to the tale.) Barring a change of venue —
requested but unlikely to be granted —
courtroom arguments should begin by early
September. Lately, and much to the
bemusement of his erstwhile colleagues at
CHP, Peyer seems to be on a "born-again"
kick. His occasional statements evince a
decided "700 Club" flavor that can only
enrich the texture and irony of the case.
The deposed officer has been hired by a
friend to do backyard swimming pool instal-
lations until the beginning of the trial
(prompting another public outcry).

The outcome of the trial seems certain, given the mammoth indictment prepared
by CHP — the great bulk of which, by the

way, has yet to be publicly released. A
source who has seen the full text of the
warrant says he sees "no way" that Peyer can
win acquittal. But journalistically speaking, this is a win-win situation. If Craig
Peyer is found guilty, then the book has its
expected denouement. If, on the other hand,
Peyer is exonerated, three intriguing questions remain to be answered: (1) What was
the significance of Peyer's unorthodox be-
havior out on the freeways? (2) Has there
been a grievous miscarriage of justice? and/
or (3) Who really killed Cara Knott, if not
Craig Peyer?

COMPETING BOOKS
None — although the nature of the
material would suggest that the project be
tackled immediately.

PROJECTED LENGTH
350 - 400 manuscript pages.

AVAILABILITY OF SOURCES
Principals on both sides are cooperat-
ing with the media. Attorney Grimes is
especially voluble, and the Knott family
seems ever willing to make public statements. Some of the outraged relatives, and
in particular the boyfriend, Wayne Bautista,
are especially "good copy."

Also, professional sources have been
contacted to help provide some perspective
on the larger questions raised by the facts
of the case: i.e., How adequate are the
screening procedures for law enforcement
hiring? What makes someone "snap"? How
well do most of us know the people we live
with, and what are some of the subtle yet
telltale signs of maladjustment?

PROJECTED MARKET

This is a true-crime book that ex-
plores a gripping, universal fear, to wit:
What happens when the system breaks down,
when the rules that make civilized life
possible no longer apply? Is there a more
heartbreaking and unexpected way to lose a
child than to a symbol of the very institution that is charged with shielding us from
such tragedy?

In Southern California, the case has
been front-page news since the day of the
killing. Even now, the most trivial new
details are accorded lead-story status on
nightly newscasts, and public interest, as
judged by letters-to-the-editor and the
like, remains voracious.

Besides the sensational crime itself,
there is the added depth of the many relationships to be examined (between Cara and
the Knotts, between Cara and her fiancé-to-
be, and, perhaps most interestingly, between
Craig and Karen Peyer) that will make read-

ers care about the characters and elevate
this story beyond the realm of "just another
murder mystery."

Overall, in terms of emotional impact,
the proposed book is a cross between The
Onion Field and Terms of Endearment — a
moving human drama with a dark, irresistible
underside.

ABOUT THE AUTHOR

A San Diego resident, Steve Salerno
has written essays and investigative pieces
for a wide spectrum of leading publications,
including Harper's, New York, the New York
Times, California, The New Republic and many
others. His first book, TNS: The Newest
Profession (Morrow, 1985), chronicled the
rise of "the new salesmanship" in America.

Due out from Morrow in November is
Salerno's first true-crime effort, Deadly
Blessing. The book is an inquiry into the
bizarre circumstances surrounding the death
of Price Daniel, Jr., reluctant scion of one
of Texas' leading political families.

Several production companies have
expressed interest in adapting the book for
television.

THREE

HOLLYWOOD'S GOLDENYEAR, 1939

This proposal sold to St. Martin's Press who published the hardcover edition of the book.

HOLLYWOOD'S GOLDEN YEAR: 1939
A Proposal for a Nonfiction Cinematic
History book

By Ted Sennett

Of all the years of Hollywood's admitted "golden" period, none was more phenomenal than 1939. At a time when the world was teetering on the edge of disaster and war clouds were forming in Europe, the studios of Hollywood combined to produce an astonishing number of films that are among the greatest and most popular of all time. Two of them, Gone With the Wind and The Wizard of Oz, were included among the ten greatest films voted in 1978 by the American Film Institute.

This book would constitute the definitive record of that glorious film year. Combining a fresh and imaginative new evaluation of each of the year's major films with a large number of carefully selected photographs, the book would have vast appeal to film lovers and film scholars, and to everyone who has ever enjoyed "going to the movies." The book would also consider the question of why this year was so productive and also look behind the scenes to discuss how these films were made.

The book would, of course, include original new evaluations of Gone With the Wind and The Wizard of Oz, but there would also be individual discussions of the following, all released in 1939:

WUTHERING HEIGHTS: Only part of the Emily Bronte novel was used, but the result was moving and magical as Laurence Olivier, Merle Oberon, and Geraldine Fitzgerald love and suffer on the brooding English moors. One of William Wyler's finest films.

GOODBYE MR. CHIPS: James Hilton's popular novel of a revered old schoolteacher was brought reverently to the screen, with Robert Donat unforgettable as Mr. Chips and Greer Garson in her American film debut as Mrs. Chips.

GUNGA DIN: Perhaps the greatest pure adventure film ever made: a lusty, enjoyable movie loosely derived from the Kipling poem, starring Cary Grant, Douglas Fairbanks, Jr., and Victor McLaglen, and featuring a truly memorable performance by Sam Jaffe in the title role.

STAGECOACH: John Ford's landmark Western took the cameras into the director's beloved Monument Valley and led John Wayne, Claire Trevor, Thomas Mitchell and a sterling cast into an exciting adventure that was also a kind of morality play.

YOUNG MR. LINCOLN: Another masterpiece from John Ford. One of the great biographical films and a brilliant piece of Americana. Ford directs Henry Fonda as the young Lincoln who grows from an awkward backwoodsman into a man of stature.

MR. SMITH GOES TO WASHINGTON: Frank Capra's irresistible political comedy-drama of a naive young man (James Stewart) who becomes a Senator and almost lives to regret it. Splendid performances by Jean Arthur, Claude Rains, and Thomas Mitchell.

NINOTCHKA: "Garbo Laughs!" the ads proclaimed — and so did audiences everywhere as the unique Greta Garbo portrayed a glum Russian official who discovers the pleasures of Paris. Ernst Lubitsch's sparkling romantic comedy, with Melvyn Douglas and Ina Claire.

DESTRY RIDES AGAIN: The rowdy Western comedy that humanized the alluring but aloof Marlene Dietrich by casting her as a music hall temptress who fights (and dies) for her man. With James Stewart and a cast brimming with expert players.

DARK VICTORY: Bette Davis gives one of her best performances as doomed heiress Judy Traherne in this poignant story. All of Warner Brother's expertise came to the fore in this superb example of shiny soap opera.

THE WOMEN: Clare Boothe Luce's scathing play was brought to the screen with most of the venom intact and a stellar MGM cast headed by Norma Shearer, Joan Crawford, Rosalind Russell, Paulette Goddard, Mary Boland, and Joan Fontaine.

LOVE AFFAIR: Charles Boyer and Irene Dunne costar in one of the screen's most beautiful love stories. Two people meet and fall in love but are separated by the whims of fate. Memorably directed by Leo McCarey.

INTERMEZZO: David O. Selznick introduced a breathtaking Swedish beauty to American audiences in this romantic drama. Her name was Ingrid Bergman, and she costarred with Leslie Howard to instant acclaim.

THE OLD MAID: Warners gave a first-rate treatment to Zoe Atkins' play about a woman (Bette Davis) who gives up her illegitimate child to her closest friend (Miriam Hopkins) and becomes the spinster aunt.

JESSE JAMES: An excellent Western drama, in Technicolor, directed by Henry King with an appreciation of American legend and history. Tyrone Power plays the whitewashed but interesting hero, with Henry Fonda as his brother Frank.

Amazingly, these were only some of the celebrated and popular films produced in 1939. Others that would be considered in detail include:

MADE FOR EACH OTHER: A moving drama of the lives, both comic and tragic, of an ordinary married couple (Carole Lombard and James Stewart).

THE STORY OF VERNON AND IRENE CASTLE: The next-to-last film starring the incomparable dance team of Fred Astaire and Ginger Rogers. A lovely valentine to America's past.

JUAREZ: An elaborate historical drama revolving about the revolutionary Mexican leader Juarez (Paul Muni), the ill-fated Emperor Maximilian (Brian Aherne), and his wife Carlotta (Bette Davis).

UNION PACIFIC: One of Cecil B. DeMille's best adventure films, centering on the building of the railroad. With Joel McCrea, Barbara Stanwyck, and a spectacular train wreck.

ONLY ANGELS HAVE WINGS: Howard Hawks' arresting melodrama about a group of mail flyers in Argentina. With Cary Grant as head pilot and Jean Arthur as the girl who learns about codes of honor and bravery.

BACHELOR MOTHER: Ginger Rogers is delightful as a resourceful shop girl who is saddled with an abandoned baby. With David Niven and Charles Coburn, and a witty screenplay.

DRUMS ALONG THE MOHAWK: John Ford's
Technicolor film recreates early American
history as Henry Fonda leads Claudette
Colbert into the hostile wilderness.

BABES IN ARMS: One of the best of the popular "Mickey-Judy" musicals, with Mickey
Rooney, Judy Garland, and a host of talented
youngsters doing justice to Rodgers and Hart
songs.

THE CAT AND THE CANARY: Bob Hope and a
haunted house are the main attractions of
this funny and frightening version of the
popular old play. With Paulette Goddard as
the lady in distress.

THE RAINS CAME: A spectacular drama set in
India, with Myrna Loy, Tyrone Power, George
Brent, and one of the most awesome climaxes
in Hollywood history.

THE HOUND OF THE BASKERVILLES: An atmo-
spheric version of Sir Arthur Conan Doyles
Sherlock Holmes melodrama, the first with
the celebrated team of Basil Rathbone and
Nigel Bruce.

ON BORROWED TIME: Paul Osborn's play about
an old man who keeps Death up a tree is
sensitively transferred to the screen, with
Lionel Barrymore as the old man and Cedric
Hardwicke as Death.

BEAU GESTE: The second and best version of
the famed adventure story of honor and
treachery in the French Foreign Legion.
With Ray Milland and Brian Donlevy.

In addition to numerous photographs,
the book would include a complete
filmography, citing credits for each of the
films discussed, an introductory essay on
the year 1939, an appendix of the awards won
by the 1939 films, and an index.

FOUR

NEW ORLEANS CREOLE COOKERY

The following is a proposal for *Creole,* by Roy F. Guste, Jr., which was sold to by Viking Studio Books, a division of Penguin-USA. Unfortunately, the book was not published.

NEW ORLEANS CREOLE COOKERY
THE DEFINITIVE WORK ON ITS HISTORY
AND DEVELOPMENT
A Proposal

By Roy F. Guste, Jr.

To understand and define the area of
cookery that is New Orleans Creole, we must
first follow the etymology of the word back
to the Latin <u>creare</u>, which means "to create
or beget." <u>Creare</u> was Franglicized into the
word <u>cria</u>, meaning "a slave brought up in
his master's house." The word "creole" is
the diminutive of <u>cria</u>.

The appelage "Creole" developed to be
used in many more expansive ways. In the
West Indies, the Spanish areas of South
America, and the French settlements of North
America the word "Creole" means "an individual of native birth but of European descent." The word "Creole" also applies to
"the white descendants of early French and
sometimes Spanish settlers of the Gulf
states who have preserved a characteristic
form of French speech and culture." Also,
the word "Creole" is used to denote "a person of mixed French and Negro or Spanish and
Negro descent speaking a dialect of French
or Spanish," used especially in Mississippi,
Alabama, and Florida.
This volume is restricted to the cuisine
developed by the Creoles of New Orleans and
their descendants, both white and black. It
is this cookery that is "New Orleans Creole
Cookery."

TABLE OF CONTENTS

      Introduction

      Notes on Illustrations
        and Photography

1.   What is "New Orleans Creole"?

2.   History of New Orleans

3.   Cultural Influences/Food Development

4.   Principal Practitioners/
      Early Restaurants

5.   Early Writers/Early Books

6.   Black Creole Cookery

7.   Creole Feasts

8.   Contemporary New Orleans Creole
      Cookery/Ongoing Development

9.   Restaurants

10.   Recipes: Classic Creole,
      Black Creole, Haute Creole,
      Contemporary Creole, Dietary Creole
      Index

CULTURAL INFLUENCE
ON THE DEVELOPMENT OF THE CUISINE

New Orleans Creole Cookery is the original indigenous American cuisine developed in and around New Orleans from the time of the city's founding in 1718. Its growth continues today.

FRENCH & FRENCH CANADIANS: The people who came to Louisiana and founded the first settlement of New Orleans were a mixture of French, Canadian French, slaves, and captured Indians. This founding group, headed

by Jean-Baptiste le Moyne, Sieur de
Bienville, first began clearing away the
canebreaks at the banks of the Saint Louis
River, now called the Mississippi after the
Indian tribe <u>Meschachebi</u>. The cooking of
that group was probably done by men who used
their knowledge of French cookery and any
improvisations they had learned in Canada.
They were a group who knew how to utilize
the natural products of the region.

   LOUISIANA INDIANS: The founding group
also included some hostile Indians who were
captured and enslaved. The most useful
culinary knowledge to Bienville was that of
these Indians who already had a cuisine
based on the plant and animal life of the
area. These Indians were the first to in-
troduce such basic products as corn to the
settlers. They used particular roots and
nuts to form the basis of their cuisine.
Corn, beans, hominy, rice, smilax root (sar-
saparilla), sagamite, groundnuts (peanuts),
hickory nuts, chestnuts, pecans, acorns,
wild sweet potatoes, arrowhead (sagittaria),
and Jerusalem artichokes were the bases of
their fare. They taught the settlers vary-
ing preparations from gruels and breads to
beverages and smoked and dried foods. One
tribe, the Natchez, had over forty different
preparations of corn alone. They were well
acquainted with the wildlife of the area and
knew many ways of hunting yet unknown to the

Frenchmen. When the colony was returned to
the possession of the French Crown by Scots-
man John Law in 1731, it became more acceptable for the French to begin migrating to
the new land and a far more affluent and
sophisticated group began to come to the
colony.

SPANISH: By 1762 the port had not
developed economically for France although
the community was thriving well. With the
Treaty of Paris in 1763, France agreed to
cede the Louisiana Territory west of the
Mississippi and the city of New Orleans to
the Spanish. This cession brought an influx
of Spaniards to the municipality and also a
strong infusion of Spanish culture and cuisine.

AFRICANS & CARIBBEAN: Throughout the
entire history of the development, from the
very beginning when those first few men
began clearing away the canebreaks along the
Mississippi for the settlement of New Orleans, slaves from both Africa and the Caribbean were a vital part of the development
of New Orleans Creole Cookery.

PRINCIPAL PRACTITIONERS

By the time of the Civil war, New
Orleans was a major American city. The
first opera house in America existed here,
where the elite of European artists would

come to perform. Mardi Gras, a traditional Catholic celebration, became a citywide festival for the occasion for the visit of the Grand Duke Alexis of Russia, who was himself in the city following the path of the exalted Jenny Lind (1772).

New Orleans was home to several of the grandest hotels in the world and certainly some of the most sophisticated restaurants that existed anywhere. One of the grand New Orleans restaurants that existed in the 1860s and still exists today is Antoine's. It was in houses like Antoine's, Monsieur Victor's, and in the dining rooms of the Saint Charles and Saint Louis Hotels that the cookery of New Orleans, Creole cookery, was served forth to travelers and citizenry, where that simple art reached new heights of perfection, where Creole became Haute Creole. The legendary Madame Begue practiced the art in her tiny single table restaurant in the French Market and gained world renown. The Crescent City had become the culinary mecca of the new world.

WRITERS AND COOKBOOKS

It was not until the 1880s that the concern for recording the existing art of Creole cookery grew into several volumes of recipes. Writers Lafcadio Hearn and Celestine Eustis, The Christian Women's

Exchange organization, and a local newspaper, The Picayune, all presented their first volumes between 1885 and 1895. Even then, although Creole cookery was soundly flourishing, there began to develop some concern for the preservation of this important legacy. Each of those works imports an aspect of Creole cookery that is peculiar to the writer and all must be taken together for one to attain comprehensive knowledge of that which had by then developed.

ILLUSTRATIONS

The illustrations for the work will be drawn from the most prestigious local collections: The Louisiana State Museum in New Orleans, The Historic New Orleans Collection, The New Orleans Public Library, the libraries of Tulane and Loyola Universities, and private collections. The graphics will include paintings, drawings, engravings, maps, historic photographs, and original color photography. I am anticipating close to 300 graphic elements: 150 in black & white and 150 in color.

There is a resurgence of interest in New Orleans Creole cookery both locally and nationally. In our city, restauranteurs are busy filling their menus with items from the cuisine that first made us the culinary mecca of the New World. Visitors to the city are now looking more and more for the true cuisine of New Orleans, instead of Nouvelle or Cajun.   There are more and more cookbooks and reprints of cookbooks on the subject appearing on the shelves, yet none come close to the work that we are discussing.

This tome is about the development not only of a form of cookery but of the most expansive, indigenous American cuisine. We are talking about a cuisine that brought the city of New Orleans through the regimes of the French and Spanish and finally to the United States. We are talking about cookery as history and culture, not as mere sustenance.

There is no work that covers the entire history of our city as it relates to our cuisine. There is no book that discusses the cultures that built this region through their respective, and subsequently common, cuisine. This is the work — this is a major American cultural contribution.

This is a book that is a necessary part of every library's cookery and food history section, along with being a history of the development of the city of New Orleans through food. This is a work that will become an integral part of the personal libraries of every student of the culinary arts, of every chef, of every lover of food and cookery.

ABOUT THE AUTHOR

Roy F. Guste, Jr. was the general
manager of Antoine's Restaurant in New Orleans, and is a fifth-generation member of
the family that owns that establishment. He
is the author of The Antoine's Restaurant
Cookbook, The Restaurants of New Orleans
Cookbook, The 100 Greatest Dishes of Louisiana Cookery, and Louisiana Light (all published by W.W. Norton).

FIVE

HOW TO WRITE AND GIVE A SPEECH

This proposal sold to St. Martin's Press, which published the hardcover edition; the trade paperback was published a year later. A revised edition has since been published and released.

HOW TO WRITE AND GIVE A SPEECH
A Practical Guide For Executives
A Proposal

By Joan Detz

The proposed book will tell everything
I know about the <u>practical</u> business of writing and giving speeches. When people read
it, they will learn in a few hours what took
me God-only-knows-how-many speech writing
assignments to learn the hard way. Lucky
readers!

THE TARGET AUDIENCE
* Primary — Business Executives
        The United States has about <u>17 million
professional and technical employees</u>, plus
about <u>7 million managers and administrators</u>.
These middle- and upper- level employees are
regularly asked to speak—at sales conferences, trade associations, professional
organizations, industry conventions, public
events.
        Most of these people are totally un-
prepared to give a speech. They didn't
learn the necessary skills in high school,
college, or even MBA programs.
        Of course, the presidents and senior
officers of major corporations hire people
to do their speech writing. But studies
show that <u>most</u> executives— more than 90
percent, in fact — must prepare their own
speeches. They are, essentially, flying
blind.

* Secondary — Politicians
        Everybody knows that the President of
the United States hires his own speech writ-

ers. So do governors, senators and other
top politicians.

But, what about the <u>300,000 lower-level
public officials</u> — county officials, mayors,
township supervisors, local council members?
These elected people can't afford to pay for
expensive speech writing services. They,
too, are flying blind.

THE NEED

The need for speech making skills is
increasing. A survey of 500 U.S. executives
found that almost 80 percent are making more
speeches now than they were a year ago.
About half say they "dread" the task.

Unfortunately, their "dread" shows. <u>A
million-plus corporate speeches are delivered each year; only a few are remembered
for more than 24 hours</u>.

Why do so many speeches fail? People
don't know how to write speeches that <u>get a
message across</u>, that <u>make an impression</u>, that
are <u>quotable</u>.

They stumble through speeches that
sound contrived. And then they wonder why
nobody listens.

THE COMPETITION

There are already some good books on
the market that tell people how to <u>deliver</u>
speeches. But, these books don't offer the
specific information that an executive needs
to <u>write</u> a memorable speech.

For example, almost all the books say, "Keep it short and simple," but they don't tell the readers HOW to keep their writing short and simple. If the readers knew exactly how to do that, they wouldn't need any book — they could be professional speech writers.

THE BENEFIT

Every product must have a benefit.

Here's what my book offers:

Readers will learn hundreds of <u>specific</u> techniques to make their speeches short and simple. They will learn <u>proven</u> ways to make their speeches lively, interesting, and memorable. They will sound more real, more human and more credible — and their audiences will be more likely to believe them.

So, for all those readers who can't afford to hire me as their personal speech writer, now there's a book that tells everything I know . . . and the readers can do it on their own.

SIX

SPONTANEOUS REMISSIONS/
BEATING THE ODDS

This proposal was used to successfully place the manuscript entitled, *Spontaneous Remissions*, with Contemporary Books. It was published in hardcover as *Beating the Odds*; the mass-market paperback edition was published by St. Martin's Press.

SPONTANEOUS REMISSIONS

A Proposal

By Albert Marchetti, M.D.

The complete proposal for the book includes this summary, a book/author sheet, a table of contents, a chapter by chapter outline, sample chapters, and supplementary material on Dr. Marchetti, including previous articles, interviews, and other pertinent biographical information.

DESCRIPTION OF THE BOOK:

The words "spontaneous remission" are utilized within the medical professions to signify the automatic and complete recovery from cancer, a sometimes unexplainable and mysterious event. These same words title Dr. Marchetti's latest book which focuses on the incredible phenomenon and employs numerous amazing real life examples to simultaneously enlighten the reader and inspire an attempt to achieve a personal remission. But more than this, <u>Spontaneous Remissions</u> logically moves the reader through an understanding of the ultimate cause of cancer and an acceptance of the ultimate cure. All information and case studies are well supported by four years of exhaustive research and an ongoing review of the world literature.

WHY THIS BOOK IS NECESSARY:

Cancer is the second worst medical killer in this country, striking new victims with each passing day. One out of every four will fall prey to this most horrifying illness and over 1.5 million new cases will develop this year alone. Even more astonishing is the thought that 40 million already carry the illness in one form or another and that about half a million sufferers will die within the year. All of these people need direction and help. More importantly, they need hope. <u>Spontaneous Remissions</u> inspirationally fills these needs.

THE INTENDED AUDIENCE:

We see three primary audiences for this book:

1. The individual who carries the diagnosis of cancer and who is searching for a successful and lasting cure.
2. The patient's family and friends who wish to help as much as possible yet lack the knowledge to do so.
3. Health conscious people who desire to educate themselves and initiate or augment a sound holistic approach to cancer prevention.

Although the audience is quite broad, it is well-defined; encompassing primarily mature adults who are direct or indirect cancer victims or otherwise generally interested in cancer prevention and cure. Consequently, the most apparent advertising media are health magazines, such as Prevention, Your Health, etc., plus other publications that cater to a health-conscious or health-crazed readership, for example, the Enquirer and the Star. In addition, health- oriented talk shows, on television and radio provide a great means of promotion with which Dr. Marchetti is already familiar.

Further, it is important to note that the many individuals who have seen portions of this book, people with and without cancer, believe that the book offers a powerful and self-applicable approach to cancer therapy. Inevitably they all wanted to read more and were very excited about the medical drama that unfolds from page to page.

THE COMPETITION:

Of course there are several cancer books on the market and some are worthy of note. These include: The Indispensable Cancer Handbook; by Kathryn H. Salsbury and Eleanor Liebman Johnson; Getting Well Again, by O. Carl Simonton, Stephanie Matthews-Simonton, and James L. Creighton; Recalled by Life, by Anthony Sattilaro; and Choices, by Marion Morra and Eve Potts.

Far and away, the best of the group is Getting Well Again by the Simontons. This book is not only authoritative and well documented, it verges on the leading edge of medical knowledge, combining conventional treatments with the most vanguard of the adjunct therapies, visualization. The Simontons are to be congratulated for a job well done. Still, there are problems with the text. It can drag and occasionally bogs down in wordy passages that tend to distract rather than stimulate the reader. To put it simply, the book is dry, from the title, Getting Well Again, to the text itself. In addition, the main thrust of the book is to present and promote the technique of visualization in the treatment of cancer — a very worthwhile endeavor but one that is somewhat limited in practice. Although the technique is effective for those who can master it, it simply is not for every one. Certainly a choice, but not a panacea.

My main criticism of Satillaro's book is that it is primarily restricted to one man's experiences, his own. And while it makes interesting reading, it is too narrow in scope. Like the Simontons, Satillaro expounds on a single treatment modality, the macrobiotic diet to which he attributes his cure. Sure, macrobiotic have a solid place

in adjunct therapy, but once again, s a
choice, not a cure-all.

The Indispensable Cancer Handbook is
actually a comprehensive guide to the latest
and best diagnosis, treatment, and supportive services for cancer patients. It is
quite different from Spontaneous Remissions
since it serves more as a compendium of
cancers, tests, therapies, and institutions;
a reference book, not a readable work designed to enlighten the inquisitive.

Choices is very much the same sort of
book. Its own description is a "handbook
designed to cover all the down-to-earth
questions people have about doctors and
hospitals, diagnosis and tests, treatments
and their side- effects, and the many options available."

In contrast, Spontaneous Remissions is
about the total and sometimes unexplainable
cure of cancer. Through numerous dramatically presented case studies, it proves that
natural healing is a definite component in
cancer recovery — at times, the only possible explanation for the cure. For people
who have cancer, it is a book that offers a
direct understanding into personal involvement in therapy and, therefore, a higher
chance for total recovery. For people
who don't have cancer, it is an exciting
examination of a dreaded disease and proof-
positive that cancer, like all other ill-

nesses, can be prevented. Collectively,
Spontaneous Remissions is a revelation
about "turning on" the natural defense system that each of us possesses.

STYLE AND TONE OF THE BOOK:

From the first chapters on, the style
and tone of the book become immediately
evident. It is a popular treatment, not one
intended to impress medical authorities and
cancer experts. It is written for the general public, specifically the cancer victim
who desperately needs the knowledge, encour-
agement, and inspiration it provides. It is
filled with incredible case studies that
pique the reader's interest and flows easily
and logically from one
topic to another. It is written in the most
concise and stimulating manner possible,
because cancer victims, like any other
critically ill individuals, don't have the
time, patience or energy to plod through a
long, dull book about their illness, regardless of how desperate they may be.

The subject matter that is presented
is also very exciting. From the concept of
spontaneous remission to the discussions of
experiments on DNA, interferon, natural
killer cells and natural cancer defense,
each topic carries the reader further down
the road of understanding and culminates in

the best means of promoting a spontaneous
remission in each individual case. Macrobiotics and visualization are certainly not
overlooked, but there are a host of other
catalysts, and they are all presented so
that the reader can tailor a specific program from the widest selection of alterna-
tives to be used in conjunction with established medical treatments.

But most importantly, the book is
inspirational in tone and style. Each case
study provides not only knowledge but also
hope. Each topic proves that we all natu-
rally possess the substances, cells, and
elements needed to bring on a remission.
Even the vocabulary, the very words used to
describe the incredible phenomenon of cancer
defense, exhilarates and motivates the
reader. The ultimate purpose of the book is
to assist in the cure, so the tone and style
are positive and uplifting.

THE AUTHOR'S CREDENTIALS:

Following a Magna Cum Laude graduation
and a Bachelor Degree in biology from Provi-
dence College, Dr. Marchetti entered the New
Jersey College of Medicine and obtained his
medical degree in 1973. His post graduate
training took place at Tampa General Hospital where he studied and practiced pathology. In 1977 he was awarded a fellowship to

the American Cancer Society and spent the
following year compiling cancer data and
lecturing to health care professionals,
predominantly Tampa-based surgeons, on a
variety of cancer topics.

In 1979, Dr. Marchetti's first book,
Common Cures For Common Ailments, was published by Stein & Day and made regional
bestseller lists around the country, following a two-month, twenty-city, talk show tour
made by the author. His second book, Dr.
Marchetti's Walking Book, was released in
1981 and was undoubtedly responsible for
much of the current interest in walking for
good health.

Dr. Marchetti has continued to write
(contributing to Cosmopolitan, Forum, Science
Digest, Boca Raton Magazine, Atlantic City
Magazine, and Florida Style, and for the past
three years has amassed a wealth of information on cancer therapy and cure, currently
being compiled into his third book, Spontaneous Remissions.

DR. MARCHETTI'S MARKETABILITY:

Dr. Marchetti has appeared on regional
television and radio talkshows in every
major market around the country. (A copy of
his last itinerary is enclosed with this
proposal.) In addition, he has given numerous printed interviews for the best newspa-

pers in the United States and has contrib-
uted to several popular national and local
magazines. He is personable, intelligent,
and articulate, and intends to be actively
involved in the promotion of the book.

SPONTANEOUS REGRESSION OF LIVER CANCER IN A
FIVE MONTH-OLD CHILD

Twenty-five years after the diagnosis
of liver cancer was made, the patient seemed
to have beaten all the odds against his
survival and was reported to be "in good
health and gainfully employed." His case
had been reviewed in a "follow-up" study
which was conducted and reported by William
J. McSweeny, M.D.; Keven E. Bove, M.D.; and
James MacAdams, M.D. from the Departments of
Radiology, Pathology and Pediatrics at the
University of Cincinnati College of Medicine. Although these fine physicians all
agreed that the child did, indeed, have a
tumor, they disagreed with the initial diagnosis of Hepatoma type liver cancer, made
when the child was first examined twenty-
five years previously. Instead, they favored Hemangioendothelioma — a blood vessel
tumor that developed within the liver.

In this particular case it is extremely important to note that the diagnoses
are significantly different. With hepatoma,
children usually die. With Hemangioendothe-

lioma, they generally live. Regardless, the
tumor was not treated because the child was
considered a hopeless case at the time.
Surprisingly, twenty-five years later the
five-month-old baby boy who had been hope-
lessly dismissed from the hospital as a
terminal cancer patient, was a grown man,
tumor free, "in good health and gainfully
employed."

WHY ?

SPONTANEOUS REGRESSION OF STOMACH CANCER
THAT HAD SPREAD TO THE LIVER

At the age of fifty-one, the patient
was admitted to Peter Bent Brigham Hospital
in Boston. He had been drinking heavily —
three- to four-fifths of whiskey each week —
and was troubled by stomach problems, weight
loss, and fatigue. A full investigation was
begun and when the patient finally went to
exploratory surgery, his doctors discovered
and removed a stomach tumor that was described as "fist size." In addition, they
removed enlarged lymph glands around the
stomach and also biopsied abnormal nodules
in the liver. The diagnosis was confirmed
by the Pathology Department — the tumor was
an adenocarcinoma of the stomach — or simply
stomach cancer.

And although the lymph glands did not
have cancer within them, a microscopic study

of the liver biopsy was positive for adenocarcinoma, just like the cancer removed from
the stomach. Obviously, the cancer had already spread and now occupied the liver.

In 1956, when this case occurred,
removing the cancer from the stomach was
considered difficult, although surgically
possible.

Removing the cancer from the liver was
known to be virtually impossible since the
more advanced techniques of radio and chemo-
therapies were virtually unknown back then.
Therefore, at the time the diagnosis was
made, the prognosis was extremely grave, and
the case was considered terminal. Then,
unexpectedly, on the tenth hospital day
after surgery, the patient developed an
infection within his abdomen and underwent a
second operation to drain an abscess that
had sprung from the stomach incision where
the cancer had been cut away. The good
news: the infection quickly cleared and the
patient left the hospital. The bad news:
although both surgeries were successful, the
patient was still doomed to die because he
still had cancer in his liver.

BUT THE PATIENT DIDN'T DIE!

Five months after his discharge from
the hospital, he had gained twenty pounds
and had returned to work symptom-free, a

hopeful sign. Three years later, however, he developed a small mass in his neck and returned to the hospital for an evaluation. Although his doctors believed that the mass represented a further manifestation of the cancer, nothing was done. The case was already considered terminal because of the liver metastases, so why put the patient through unnecessary discomfort in his last days.

Then circumstances began to change. Two years after the neck mass developed, it mysteriously and spontaneously disappeared. Later, in 1968, twelve years after the double surgeries, the patient seemed totally cured. While undergoing unrelated gall bladder surgery for gallstones, the patient was completely reexamined inside and out and was found to be totally free of cancer. No nodules in the liver! No recurrent cancer in the stomach! No cancer in the neck! No cancer whatsoever was discovered!

After reviewing the case and examining all the reports, slides, lab work, and X-rays, M.D.s Steven A. Rosenberg, Edward Fox, and Winthroup H. Churchill of the National Cancer Institute in Bethesda, Maryland, submitted their report to Cancer Magazine. It was published in February of 1972. They concluded "that the patient provides evidence that the regression of hepatic

metastases from stomach cancer can occur
without therapy." Then added that "the
cause of such regression is unknown."

W H Y ?

REGRESSION OF CANCER FOLLOWING MEASLES
INFECTION.

In this case the patient was a eight-
year-old African boy who entered Mulago
Hospital on December 1, 1970, with a form of
cancer known as Burkitts Lymphoma — a ma-
lignant conditions of the lymph glands.

The case was reported in the July 10,
1971, issue of <u>The Lancet</u>, a highly respected
British medical journal. And the work was
supported by contract numbers PH 43-67-1343
and PH 43-6767 from the National Cancer
Institute in Bethesda, Maryland.

The case is extremely well documented
and very often cited. At the time of admission, the lymphoma tumor was growing behind
the child's right eye, causing displacement,
blindness, and paralysis of the eye. A
biopsy of the tumor was performed and when
the abnormal tissue was prepared and examined under a microscope it was described as
Burkitts Lymphoma, a horrible form of cancer.

Luckily for the child, on December 13,
before any kind of therapy could be initi-

ated, he caught the measles. Also recorded on that same day, his doctors noted that the tumor behind his eye began reducing in size. After just two weeks of recovery, not only had the measles cleared, but the tumor had totally disappeared. Completely and without any form of therapy, the child was totally cured.

Apparently there was a connection between the infection and the disappearance of the tumor. Did the measles virus attack the tumor cells? Did the body's reaction to the measles also provoke a reaction to the tumor? Was it fever, antibodies, interferon, or steroids produced and released from the adrenal glands?

Avrum Z. Blumberg and John L. Zeigler who reported this case from the Uganda Cancer Institute at Kampala, Uganda, were uncertain about the relationship between the measles and the tumor but they were convinced that the child was totally free of cancer.

W H Y ?

CONTENTS

Preface

Acknowledgments

Introduction

The Spontaneous
Remission of Cancer

I: HOW HEALING WORKS

  2 The Process of Healing

  3 Conventional Therapy

  4 What You Need to Know
     About Cancer

  5 The Natural Defense System

  6 The Link Between the Mind
     and the Body

II: YOUR BODY HEALER

  7 Macrobiotics and the
     Remission of Cancer

  8 Exercise and the
     Remission of Cancer

III: YOUR MENTAL HEALER

  10 Meditation and the
      Remission of Cancer

  11 Visualization and the
      Remission of Cancer

  12 Hypnosis and the
      Remission of Cancer

IV: COMBINING THERAPIES
  13   Metabolic Therapies and the
       Remission of Cancer
  14   Crossing the Finish Line
  15   Another Winner
       Bibliography
       Index

FORMATTING / STYLE SAMPLE

THE KILLER'S GAME

Some books are great. This is one great book.
—PM

Page 1

P M A

LITERARY AND FILM MANAGEMENT, INC.

THE KILLER'S GAME

(Formerly THE GODFORSAKEN)

A Novel of Suspense

By

Jay R . Bonansinga

(To be published by Simon & Schuster,

Spring '97)

© All Rights Reserved

Page 2

PART I:

SLUGGER GETS A HIT

"Learn what you are and be such"

- Pindar

Odes

ONE

The clinic was in a low slung, nonde-
script building at the corner of LaSalle
and Huron, and the gunmetal Chicago sky
was just starting to look threatening as
Joseph Riley Flood arrived for his 9:00
AM appointment. He went inside and gave
his name to the receptionist. She directed him into a small examination room
just off the lobby.

          Joe sat down on a cold laminate
chair and stewed for a moment, wanting to
be anywhere else. Arms folded, thick
shoulders straining the seams of his
houndstooth sport coat, he had the air of
a hard-ass coach about him, an old jock
whose muscles had congealed into hard
fat, whose ruddy complexion and henna
brown hair were getting grayer every day.
He still had <u>the smile</u>, though. The
killer Irish smile. He could still light
fires with that damn thing.

Trouble was, Joe hadn't been smiling very much lately. Just a couple of weeks ago, he had suffered through his fiftieth birthday, and it had put a real zap on his head. Never mind that his body was coming apart at the seams and never mind that he couldn't get within twenty feet of his favorite spicy foods anymore, and never mind that his eyesight was starting to go; the worst part was the simple mathematics of it. Wilt Chamberlain retired in 1974 at the age of thirty-eight, and he was considered a goddamned senior citizen. Jimmy Conners played in the U.S. Open in his forties, and he was considered a freak. Joe didn't like the ring of fifty years old one little bit.

A nurse materialized out of nowhere and started prepping Joe's arm for the needle. Told him she needed to take another sample of Joe's blood. "They did that already," Joe informed her.

THE
FICTION
PROPOSAL

THE JERSEY DEVIL

The following essay was originally published by *Atlantic City* Magazine and was used to propose a concept for a fiction trilogy that was successfully placed with Lynx Books. The author wrote the first novel (his writing style was compared to that of Anne Rice, Richard Condon and Nathaniel West). Unfortunately, Lynx Books filed for bankruptcy and the novel was not published.

THE JERSEY DEVIL

An Essay

By Christopher Cook Gilmore

MEET THE JERSEY DEVIL
At last, the real story about
the wayward son who ate his family

DO NOT BE ALARMED. The only person who knows
the whole truth aboout the Jersey Devil, his
mother, has been dead for almost 200 years.
She has nothing to say. She is dead and the
Devil lives, and the rest is lies.

Mother Leeds was not her real name.
It was Tatiwawaruntu, or Head of Stone, and
she was a full-blooded Lenni-Lenape Indian.
When she was fourteen her parents were found
roasted alive in an old, abandoned Indian
roaster near Batsto. Blamed for the tragedy
and banished from her tribe, she slept in
the pines until a family of early settlers
named Leeds took her in and married her to
one of their men, Zebedee Leeds, sixty-
five, a widower and a deaf-mute. They all
lived on Leeds point in the Pine Barrens, a
very weird place in 1778.

New Jersey is easily the weirdest
state in the Union, and back then the Leeds
people were definitely the weirdest in the
state. They were pure Piney, crazy enough,
but on top of that they lived for generations on remote parts of Great Bay so thick
with rats, gnats, flies, and mosquitoes it
could drive anyone mad. Methane gas rotted
their brains, while poverty, inbreeding,
and bad whiskey finished off their souls.

No wonder that one of them, sooner or later, would spawn a devil.

The legend is that Mother Leeds, as she came to be called, was a witch, which she was, and that her husband was a warlock, which is a lie. Zebedee Leeds never knew what was going on. Blinded by lightning on his wedding night, he lived another 15 years, long enough to father a dozen children. He was drowned in the bay and consumed by spider crabs. A year later his widow gave birth to her 13th child. She swore on the Leeds Bible that Satan had come to her in the night in the form of an animal, a big flatfish, and seduced her. Because she was the daughter of a medicine an, she was believed. The baby was a boy, and she called him Son.

The story goes that on his thirteenth birthday, in the middle of a griddle-cake party, Son ate his mother. He then ate his twelve brothers and sisters. Appetite appeased, he sprouted wings, horns and a tail, flew up the chimney and took off for the pines. He is seen to this day running around the treetops with his feet on fire and howling from the pain. He is blamed for everything that goes wrong: barnyard mutants, vegetable freaks, chain-saw malfunctions, anything at all. Son Leeds, goes the story, never leaves New Jersey. He can't stand the climate, and that is why they call him the Jersey Devil.

The truth is that Mother Leeds and her first twelve children all died natural deaths, mostly by fire, flood, or quicksand. A few of their descendants still live on the marshes, but most of them moved back to the pines. They go to church and can read and write. Today the Devil has no more interest in them than he has in anyone else. Son Leeds, whose real father was a deserter from the British Army, was strikingly handsome and extremely intelligent. A skilled angler, he spent most of his life drifting for flounder on the bay. Son was no demon, but he certainly was a devil with the ladies. A bachelor till he died, he had nine-two girlfriends, all of them with gentle natures and wonderful figures. Son's amorous exploits became legendary, which is probably at the bottom of everything. Some say Son's spirit passed into future generations, and that this spirit, which exists in many a Jersey boy, is the Jersey Devil. Jersey girls say he comes to them at night, usually in nightclubs, and asks them to dance. They say it's their sweet selves he wants, not their souls, and that what he likes most is to take them fishing. Some girls say he looks like an old yellow dog, some like a wildcat.

And some say he looks a lot like me.

THE
TELEVISION
SERIES
PROPOSAL

ONE

TRUE MURDER MYSTERIES

This proposal was written for a syndicated television series that was optioned to Atlantic Kushner-Locke. The option lapsed after a year; the project was reoptioned to King World. My partner, Vincent Bugliosi, and I wrote the accompanying presentation script, hoping it would increase our chances of selling the series. After King World's option lapsed, the project was optioned to The Ventura Entertainment Group. Currently, we are working on placing this project.

THE FIRST RUN
SYNDICATED OR NETWORK
TELEVISION SERIES
AND PRESENTATION SCRIPT

TRUE MURDER MYSTERIES

A HALF-HOUR, OR HOUR TELEVISION DRAMA
COMPILED FROM TRUE MURDER MYSTERIES

To be narrated by Vincent T. Bugliosi

Created by:
Vincent T. Bugliosi and Peter Miller

Executive Producers:
Vincent T. Bugliosi and Peter Miller

PRODUCTION NOTES

Each episode will examine one of the most
famous, colorful, and significant murder
cases in the annals of American crime, ones
where an element of mystery, to this very
day, endures. The producers have done extensive research as to which murders qualify
for this programming, and include a few
dozen examples of suggested cases hereafter.

INTRODUCTION

Each half hour will begin with an introduction by Vincent Bugliosi, in a courtroom
setting, giving a brief summary of the case,
including its cast of characters, i.e., the
accused, the victim, the witnesses, etc.
Where possible, the actual scene of the
crime will be shown, and film footage and/or
interviews with those involved will be in-
corporated into this segment.

THE ACCUSED

Basing his account on official records and
all other available information, Mr. Bugliosi will then give the background of the
accused, including a psychological portrait
of him and his relationship, if any, with
the victim. This background and portrait
will help the viewer form an opinion as to
whether or not the accused did, in fact,
commit the murder, and if so, what his mo-

tive was. Photographs and film footage of
the accused, where available, will be shown
during the segment.

THE MURDER

Next, each show will dramatically recreate
the murder (including the known events leading up to and following the murder), allowing the audience to become an eyewitness to
the crime. At the end of this scene, Mr.
Bugliosi will appear at the scene of the
crime ("breaking walls"), and will then
reveal the events leading up to the arrest
of the accused murderer.

THE EVIDENCE
[PHYSICAL AND SCIENTIFIC]

We will then proceed with an examination of
the evidence in the case. Where available,
the actual murder weapon will be revealed to
the viewing audience. In this segment, Mr.
Bugliosi will analyze the key evidence, such
as fingerprints, firearm identification
(popularly but erroneously referred to as
ballistics), blood and hair comparisons,
etc. In examining this evidence, Mr. Bugliosi will utilize the official investigative documents in the case, such as police
and autopsy reports.

THE TRIAL

Highlights of the trial will then be recre-
ated. This segment may consist of the direct examination, cross- examination, and
final summation, utilizing excerpts from the
actual trial transcript.

THE SUMMATION

We will close each program with a summation
by Mr. Bugliosi in which he sets forth the
results of the trial and the sentence of the
accused (if there was a conviction). In the
event any new evidence surfaced subsequent
to the trial, Mr. Bugliosi will detail how
such evidence might have affected the verdict if it had been offered at the trial.
He will close his presentation with thought-
provoking observations about the case and
the evidence and, finally, will render his
own verdict as to whether . . . Justice Has
Been Served.

TRUE MURDER MYSTERIES

Suggested Case List

1. THE BORDEN MURDER MYSTERY (Fall River,
Mass., 1892). Ax murders of Borden's father
and stepmother. Borden acquitted despite
strong evidence.

2. THE DEATH OF STANFORD WHITE (New York,
1906). Eminent architect shot by Harry

Thaw, the pathologically jealous husband of a former lover.

3. THE POLITICS AND DEATH OF SACCO AND VANZETTI (South Braintree, Mass., 1920). Italian immigrants found guilty and electrocuted for the murder of two payroll couriers.

4. FATTY ARBUCKLE: A CRUSH ON A GIRL (San Francisco, 1921). Weighty screen comic Arbuckle accused of crushing starlet Virginia Rappe as he raped her. Arbuckle was acquitted.

5. THE HOLLYWOOD MYSTERY (Los Angeles, 1922). Unsolved slaying of a respected actor and film director.

6. LEOPOLD AND LOEB: THRILL KILL (Chicago, 1924). Rich youths murder a boy for the adrenaline thrill of killing.

7. THE BUNGLING LOVERS MYSTERY (Long Island, 1927). Two lovers clumsily bludgeon a husband to death, each blaming the other in court.

8. THE HAWAIIAN HOMICIDE (Honolulu, 1931). One of a group of Japanese-Hawaiians accused of raping Thalia Massie is executed in racially-motivated vengeance.

9. THE LINDBERGH BABY MYSTERY (New Jersey, 1932). Aviator's son is stolen from crib and murdered, then ransomed by Bruno Hauptmann.

10. THE QUESTION OF DR. SAM SHEPARD (Cleveland, 1954). While blaming an unknown killer, a doctor is found guilty of murdering his wife. Newspaper sensationalism leads to retrial and acquittal.

11. JUDGE, JURY, AND EXECUTIONER (Florida, 1955). Fearing that his corruption will be exposed, Judge Joseph Peel arranges the death of a noted colleague.

12. PERRY SMITH & RICHARD HICKOCK: KILLERS "IN COLD BLOOD"
(Holcomb, Kansas, 1959). Ex-cons butcher a farmer and his family, thinking money is hidden in the house. Basis for In Cold Blood.

13. DEATH AND THE SWINGING DOCTOR (Los Angeles, 1959). Dr. Bernard Finch and his lover murder the doctor's wife, surviving.

14. THE BOSTON STRANGLER MYSTERY (Boston, 1962). Albert DeSalvo confesses to the sex slayings of thirteen Boston women.

15. CANDY AND MELVIN (Florida, 1964). Blonde bombshell conspires with her boyfriend to

murder her husband. Brilliant defense leads
to her acquittal.

16. THE ALICE CRIMMINS CASE (New York,
1965). Two small children are murdered by
their mother, who claims it was the work of
kidnappers.

17. THE RICHARD SPECK MASS MURDERS (Chicago,
1966). Psychopath murders eight nurses in a
single night in a Chicago hotel.

18. JAMES EARL RAY: THE MARTIN LUTHER KING
ASSASSINATION (Memphis, 1968). Ray fires a
rifle shot that kills black civil rights
leader, Martin Luther King, Jr.

19. SIRHAN SIRHAN: THE ARAB FANATIC (Los
Angeles, 1968). Sirhan guns down Robert
Kennedy in a hotel kitchen on the night he
wins the California presidential primary.

20. DEATH IN HOUSTON HIGH SOCIETY (Houston,
1969-72). A wealthy socialite is ostensibly
poisoned by her doctor husband who, in turn,
is shot by a paid killer.

21. MANSON (Los Angeles, 1969). Charismatic
guru leads a group of followers to vicious
murders. Basis for the book Helter Skelter.

22. THE GREEN BERET MURDERS (Ft. Bragg,
North Carolina, 1971). A doctor claims hippies

broke into his house and stabbed his wife
and daughters. Convicted nine years later.

23. THE MYSTERY OF THE MURDERED MIGRANTS
(Yuba City, California, 1971). Over a period of weeks in the early Spring, Juan
Corona slaughters twenty-five migrant work-
ers, burying them in shallow graves.

24. THE HOPE MASTERS CASE (California,
1972). After murdering her lover, a charm-
ing killer persuades a woman to fall in love
with him.

25. THE MYSTERY OF THE MURDERED MOTHER (Con-
necticut, 1973). Wrongly convicted of killing his mother, a boy wins his freedom with
the help of dedicated neighbors.

26. THE "MAN IN BLACK" MYSTERY (Ft. Worth,
Texas, 1976). A "man in black" murders millionaire Cullen Davis's stepdaughter and
wife's lover. Davis was acquitted.

27. QUESTIONS ABOUT BUDDY (New York, 1978).
In a fit of jealousy, a noted horse trainer
murders his ex- girlfriend's new lover.

28. AN EVIL WITHIN: THE REINERT MYSTERY
(Pennsylvania, 1979). A rich schoolteacher
and her children are killed, both for re-
venge and for their insurance money.

29. THE DEATH OF JOHN SINGER (Utah, 1979). A man making a moral stand by keeping his children from school is shot by sheriff's deputies.

30. THE ENIGMA OF JEAN HARRIS (Purchase, New York, 1980). Dr. Herman Tarnower is shot by his mistress, who claims the shooting occurred as Tarnower tried to prevent her suicide.

31. DARK DAYS FOR SUNNY (Rhode Island, 1980). An heiress falls into a coma, presumably after a murderous insulin injection is administered by her husband.

32. TRANSSEXUAL TROUBLE (New York, 1981). After a sex change operation, a woman is murdered at the hands of two former lovers: one gay, one heterosexual.

33. THE BLACK MASK MURDER (New York, 1985). An apparent desire for necrophilic homosexual sex leads to the murder of a Norwegian male model.

34. THE BENSON BOMB MURDERS (Naples, Florida, 1985). Heir to a tobacco fortune plants two pipe bombs in the family car, killing his mother and another family member.

35. THE MORMON MYSTERY (Salt Lake City,
1985). Master forger of historic Mormon
archives murders two people to avoid exposure.

THE BORDEN MURDER MYSTERY
(Sample Murder Synopsis)

On the oppressively hot morning of August 4, 1892, in Fall River, Massachusetts, Andrew J. Borden, sixty-nine, a prosperous and dictatorial banker, and his second wife, Abby, forty-two, were found murdered by savage blows to the head; their faces hacked to pieces and nearly unrecognizable. Suspicion soon fell on Borden's daughter Lizzie, a thirty-two-year-old spinster and Sunday school teacher. Lizzie shared a modest two-story house with her father, step-mother, a maid, and her sister, Emma. Emma and Lizzie — their natural mother having died when Lizzie was two — didn't seem to like their step-mother: they referred to her only as "Mrs. Borden." On the day before the killings, a visiting uncle arrived and found the elder Bordens doubled over with severe stomach pains. It was later discovered that Lizzie had that day purchased a vial of prussic acid, a poison, though no connection was established. Also, on the evening of the 3rd, Lizzie suddenly became clairvoyant, predicting violence and disaster for the Borden family. Early the next day, Emma set off to visit friends in a nearby town, Uncle John Vinnicum Morse went for a long walk, and Mr. Borden left to make some business calls. Mrs. Borden, busied by household tasks, told Bridget, the maid, to wash the windows. When Mr. Borden

returned home later, he inquired as to the
whereabouts of his wife.   Lizzie explained
that Mrs. Borden had left the house, telling
Lizzie she received a note from a sick friend
requesting help.   Tired, Mr. Borden lay down
in the sitting-room to rest.   An hour later,
the maid was awakened from a nap by Lizzie's
shriek, "Bridget! Come down quick! Someone's
killed father!"   The maid also found the body
of Mrs. Borden in the guest room.   Medical
evidence later proved that Mrs. Borden had
been slain an hour to an hour and a half before
Mr. Borden.   Lizzie was arrested on August 11.
Beyond her obvious enmity toward her step mother,
other evidence weighed against Lizzie.   No one
would appear to confirm her story of the sick-
note from a friend, she never gave consistent
answers about her whereabouts at the time of
the murders, she burned a possibly bloodstained
dress three days after the deaths, and there
were the prussic acid and the premonitions.
Her trial began nearly a year later, on June 1,
1893.   Her attorney, a former governor of the
commonwealth, defended her mainly by contrast-
ing the gruesomeness of the murders with Lizzie's
calm and refined demeanor.   How could a Sunday
school teacher, a leader in Christian and tem-
perance leagues, a sensitive art fancier, a
delicate-looking young woman, ever have committed these heinous crimes?   On June 13, la-
dylike Lizzie Borden sat with her pince-nez
perched on her nose and was acquitted.   With

her sister, she inherited an estate worth half a million dollars in modern terms, and lived comfortably to an old age.

THE TELEVISION
SYNDICATED OR NETWORK SERIES
PRESENTATION SCRIPT

TRUE MURDER MYSTERIES

Presentation Script
Created By
Vincent T. Bugliosi & Peter Miller

OPENING SHOT:

EXT: STREET—DAY

It is the scene of a crime. Police and medics
are all busy with their various tasks. As the
body is placed in the ambulance and the door is
slammed, VINCENT T. BUGLIOSI walks into the
scene. He looks down at the chalk outline of a
body and then up at the camera.

> BUGLIOSI
>
> "Thou Shalt Not Kill." The Fifth Com-
> mandment. Murder has, throughout man's
> history, been viewed as the most hei-
> nous crime of all, the one act by
> another human being we all fear the
> most. Yet paradoxically, despite its
> horror, we are endlessly fascinated by
> it, particularly when there's an
> element of mystery. Perhaps it's
> because of the innate desire we all
> have to play the part of the detec-
> tive. Or perhaps the reason is that
> most important element of murder,
> death, is itself shrouded in mystery!
> In our never-ending effort to solve the
> mystery of death, we are inescapably
> attracted to it.

Mr. Bugliosi walks off screen.

EXT: L.A. COUNTY COURTHOUSE—DAY

Mr. Bugliosi walks into the scene.

                    BUGLIOSI

In the past, men looked to primitive
codes of justice to provide the solu-
tions to crimes.   Today, we have a vast
and impressive legal system which we
rely on to bring criminals to justice.
Yet, it is an imperfect system and not
every case can be solved completely and
satisfactorily.

Mr. Bugliosi begins walking up the stairs.

                    BUGLIOSI

Come with me now as I investigate some
of the most mysterious murder cases of
our time and ask the fundamental question:

Mr. Bugliosi pauses at the door.

                    BUGLIOSI

Are we satisfied beyond a reasonable
doubt that we know the truth?

Mr. Bugliosi walking into the building.

Credits role . . .   TMM theme music plays.

XYZ Production Company Presents

TRUE MURDER MYSTERIES

Hosted By

Vincent T. Bugliosi

Created By

Vincent T. Bugliosi

&

Peter Miller

Mr. Bugliosi enters the courtroom, puts his coat
down at the prosecutor's table, walks up to the
Judge's bench and stands.

BUGLIOSI

Hello, I'm Vincent Bugliosi. Some of
you may know me as the Deputy District
Attorney of Los Angeles County who
prosecuted Charles Manson and members
of his family for the infamous Tate-
LaBianca murders. Or you may have
read my book about that case called
Helter Skelter. In that particular
case I was able to clearly prove
Manson's guilt beyond all reasonable
doubt even though Manson didn't per-
sonally commit any of the murders for
which he was convicted. In other trials the outcome, whether guilty or not
guilty is not always clear. For in-

stance, I'm sure you've all heard of
Lizzie Borden. The well- known limerick
about her goes:
Lizzie Borden took an axe, And gave her
mother forty whacks. When she saw what
she had done, She gave her father forty-
one.
But, how many of you know that actually
she was found not guilty, despite
strong, circumstantial evidence
against her? Why is this? In TRUE
MURDER MYSTERIES we will see that an
explanation for at least some of such
cases is that the alternate legal issue
at a criminal trial is not whether or
not the accused committed the crime,
but whether the prosecution was able
to prove that he did <u>beyond a reason-</u>
<u>able doubt</u>. In American jurisprudence,
then, a verdict of "Not Guilty" is not
always synonymous with "Innocence."

Mr. Bugliosi walks around to the witness chair
and takes a seat.

                    BUGLIOSI
Or look at the case of Claus von Bulow,
the man who was charged, in 1981, with
the attempted murder of his wife,
Sunny. After an initial conviction he
was later acquitted in another trial
despite the existence of evidence
which had proven him guilty at the

first trial. How did two juries hearing the same case arrive at two completely different conclusions?

Mr. Bugliosi stands and walks up to a series of
enlarged newsprint type black & white photographs
and headlines of the Lizzie Borden case, the
Lindbergh case, the von Bulow trial, and an even
larger spread for the Kennedy assassination.

[Note: A well lit and carefully designed, durable
presentation of famous murders can be designed
for this production, and also used for other
presentation purposes, i.e., N.A.P.T.E.]

BUGLIOSI
The Murders that we will choose to
examine in our series, TRUE MURDER
MYSTERIES, will all have a specific
element of mystery surrounding them,
which endures to this very day. Since
there is a vast library of fascinating
cases from which to choose, we'll have
an inexhaustible supply of murder
mysteries. Some of the cases we will
explore in our show have been well
publicized. Many have not. All will
captivate you, the viewer.

With each one-hour presentation, I will
begin by giving a brief summary of the
case, including sharing photographs
and, where available, film footage of
the cast of characters, that is, the

accused, the victim, the witnesses, etc
. . . Where possible, the actual scene
of the crime will be shown to the
viewing audience.

Based on official records and all other
available information, I will then give
the background of the accused, including a psychological portrait of him and
his relationship, if any, with the
victim. This background and portrait
will help the viewer form an opinion as
to whether or not the accused did, in
fact, commit the murder, and if so, what
his motive was.

Next, each show will dramatically recreate the murder, including the known
events immediately leading up to and
following the murder, thereby allowing
the audience to become an eyewitness to
the crime.

We will then proceed with an examination of the evidence in the case.
Where available, the actual murder
weapon will be shown to the viewing
audience. In this segment, from the
official investigative documents in the
case, I will analyze the key evidence,
such as fingerprints, firearm identification, blood and hair comparisons,

incriminating statements and conduct,
etc . . . It's at this point that I
will discuss questions and mysteries in
the case that to this day remain unan-
swered, and evidence, some of it new,
which cries out for a second look.
TRUE MURDER MYSTERIES will give the
viewers the opportunity to examine all
of the evidence themselves and draw
their own conclusions.

The next segment will be a capsulized
recreation of the trial. It will consist of the highlights of the direct
examination, cross-examination and
final summation, utilizing excerpts
from the actual trial transcripts.

Finally, in each drama I will give a
summation in which I set forth results
of the trial and the sentence of the
accused if there was a conviction. I
will then discuss how the new evidence,
if any, and the enduring mysteries
about the case, if answered, might have
affected the verdict. I will close the
presentation with thought-provoking
observations about the case and the
evidence.

INT: LIBRARY—DAY (Note: either a home library or
public)

Mr. Bugliosi enters the scene and takes a seat in
a comfortable armchair. From a table by the
chair he picks up a book. Behind him the walls
are lined with hundreds of books on crime, e.g.,
Helter Skelter, In Cold Blood, Fatal Vision,
Murder At The Met, A Cast Of Killers, etc.

                  BUGLIOSI

When I first became fascinated with the
concept of creating TRUE MURDER MYSTER-
IES, I realized that even though other
crime anthology programming exists on
television, no series has ever dealt
specifically with the myriad of true
murder mysteries of twentieth-century
North American history. Another plus for
TRUE MURDER MYSTERIES is the fact that
murder mysteries are a major staple in
our nation's entertainment
industries...from books like In Cold
Blood and Presumed Innocent, to TV
miniseries like The Nutcracker and The
Billionaire Boys Club, and major feature
films like The Jagged Edge and Suspect.
So there's obviously a large audience
for this type of story, most of which
are fictional. If fictional murder
mysteries have a mass appeal, then
TRUE MURDER MYSTERIES will prove to be
that much more intriguing to the viewing public. The incredible nature of
many of the murder mysteries we will
examine in our series will prove once

again that real life is, indeed,
stranger than fiction.

Mr. Bugliosi stands and puts his book back on the
shelf.

> BUGLIOSI
> Now, ladies and gentlemen, I will offer
> a sampling of some of the murder cases.

INT: MIAMI BEACH MANSION—DAY

Mr. Bugliosi walks into a posh foyer and pauses
on the stairwell.

> BUGLIOSI
> On June 30, 1964, multi-millionaire
> Jacques Mossler was bludgeoned to death
> in his mansion in Miami. Oddly
> enough, Mossler's wife, Candy, had gone
> out driving at 1:00 a.m. with their four
> children. By the time she returned at
> 4:30 a.m., her husband was dead.
> Later, investigators discovered that
> Candy's nephew, Melvin, had flown from
> Houston to Florida and back within 24
> hours of the murder. Then, Melvin was
> linked to the murder weapon, and his
> palm print was discovered on the
> kitchen counter. The State even pro-
> duced two ex-cons who claimed that
> Candy and Melvin had offered them money
> to kill Mossler. All of this circum-
> stantial evidence was enough to war-
> rant a trial for Candy and Melvin, but
> it wasn't enough to convict them.

What had seemed like a convincing case
evaporated under the heat of the
defense's brutal attack on Mr.
Mossler's character, and the allegation
that there were others who had a motive
and opportunity for killing Mossler.
Candy and Melvin were acquitted.

INT: ELLIS ISLAND. THE EMPTY HALLS OF THE WEL-
COME CENTER — DAY

Mr. Bugliosi walks through the rooms, the New
York skyline or the Statue of Liberty seen
through the windows.

                    BUGLIOSI
On August 23, 1927, two Italian immigrants who had been convicted of murder were electrocuted in Massachusetts
seven years after what is still one of
the most controversial trials in history: the trial of Sacco and
Vanzetti. They were charged in the
shooting death and robbery of two
couriers who were transferring $16,000.
The evidence against the men was slim
at the outset, but witnesses' memories
mysteriously improved during the year
prior to the trial when Sacco and
Vanzetti's radical politics surfaced.
At the time, the U.S. Attorney General
and the immigration service were engaged
in a campaign to rid America of all
immigrants who held "subversive" po-

litical beliefs. Webster Phair, the
presiding judge, made no effort to
conceal his distaste for the immigrants, repeatedly referring to them
out of court as "wops" and "dagos."

Sacco and Vanzetti were found guilty
and subsequently electrocuted. But how
much of a role did political and racial
bias play in the determination of their
guilt and innocence? Ten years ago,
the Commonwealth of Massachusetts, in
an unusual move, formally acknowledged
that Sacco and Vanzetti "did not receive a fair trial."   This was not,
however, a concession of their innocence. Were they, in fact, guilty?

EXT: OPEN FIELD, New Brunswick, N.J. — DAY

Mr. Bugliosi stands near an apple tree. It is
September 14, 1922.

Some period 1920's cars drive by. Under the
tree, a man and a woman are dead.

> BUGLIOSI
> A little over two years after the kill-
> ing we just discussed occurred, a
> murder took place in New Brunswick, New
> Jersey, which was so fascinating that
> in 1950, a special issue of LIFE MAGA-
> ZINE labeled the Hall-Mills murder the
> "Crime of the Half Century." On the
> morning of September 14, 1922, the

dead bodies of Reverend   Edward Wheeler
Hall of St. John the Evangelist Church
and his lover, Eleanor Mills, a married
member of the church choir, were discovered   neatly arranged under a tree,
with Eleanor's head resting on the
minister's right arm.   Edward's genita-
lia were placed in his mouth and several love letters were strewn around on
the ground.   Despite a lengthy and
highly controversial trial in which
the Reverend's wife and his lover's
two brothers were charged with the
murders, the case was never solved, all
of these defendants being found not
guilty. To this very day, theories
abound as to who the real murderer, or
murderers, are. Yet another mystery in
the annals of American crime history.

NOTE: We can add other murder descriptions here,
depending on how long the presentation tape will
be. Those murders could include Charles
Lindbergh's baby, John F. Kennedy, Martin Luther
King, Jr., the Dr. Sam Shepard case, et al. Also
note that we now need specific directions, i.e.:
What the budget is? How long is it going to be?
Hour? Half Hour?

INT: COURTROOM—DAY

Mr. Bugliosi is back at the counsel's table.

BUGLIOSI

Ladies and gentlemen, thank you for
viewing this brief presentation. I hope
I've piqued your interest about what I
believe to be a ready-made marketability
of TRUE MURDER MYSTERIES, a provoca-
tive, perceptive, and yes, educational
examination of the most intriguing
cases in the annals of American crime.

Vince gathers up some legal books.

FADE OUT: THE END

TWO

THE INSIDE MAN

The following proposal and treatment is for a network television movie of the week (MOW) and one hour dramatic series. This presentation is presently being offered to producers and networks in the hopes of making a development deal for the movie and/or the series production. Often time movies of this kind are referred to as "back door pilots" in that they serve first as an MOW and then as a vehicle for defining the cast of an eventual series.

THE INSIDE MAN

By Jerry Schmetterer

A Proposal for a Television Movie

There is a problem inside Attica. And
Dave Lewis knows that if he doesn't solve it
soon, New York State will lose control of
its toughest prison.

For months Lewis, Inspector General of
the State Department of Correction, has been
getting letters from an Attica inmate named
Lester Osborne, a three time loser serving a
life sentence without possibility of parole
for the murder of a schoolteacher. In his
letters Osborne tells Lewis of a new gang
inside the prison. Osborne says the gang is
not like the others that are common in all
prisons: gangs of blacks, Hispanics, Indians, bikers, or homosexuals, banded together
for protection against their natural en-
emies. Instead, Osborne hints strongly that
this new gang is a gang of white suprema-
cists, not unusual in Southern or Western
prisons but so far unknown in New York's
system. But Osborne insists that there is
something about this gang that makes it more
dangerous than any other — it is made up of
the correction officers themselves. The
guards have become a criminal entity.
Osborne says he will tell more if Lewis can
help him get his sentence changed; he wants
a chance at parole.

Osborne's letters are not unusual.
Inmates often try to help Lewis — who is
responsible for the honesty and integrity of
the civil servants who run the system (simi-

lar to the internal affairs of a police
department) in exchange for some special
treatment.

Lewis is in charge of a very small
department comprising only a dozen or so
investigators and clerks. His position is
really a political appointment, made traditionally by governors in order to keep
prison reformers off their backs. Lewis has
neither the staff nor the time to act
quickly on things, but Osborne's letters
strike an alarming note; they send up a red
flag in Lewis' mind.

Lewis is most bothered by the possibility that prison guards have joined together in a conspiracy. This could be a
very dangerous situation. It would mean
that the guards, not the state department of
prisons, were running the institution.
There is no doubt in Lewis' mind that this
could happen — it had happened in the past,
always with devastating results to the penal
system. The lowest guards always really
knew more about the goings-on inside the
prison walls than the warden. If they decided to walk on the other side of the law,
guards could in effect turn the prison over
to the most powerful inmates. They could
smuggle drugs for them, aid in escape, run
criminal errands outside the walls — guards
had even committed murder at the order of
prisoners they worked for.

What made this case so potentially dangerous was Osborne's discussion of the guard's white supremacist motives. The Aryan Brotherhood had long existed among prison inmates throughout the country. Comprised mainly of white, violent inmates, it was ostensibly a means of white prisoners protecting themselves from the black and Latino gangs. In reality, the Aryan Brotherhood was as violent and aggressive as any of the black or Latino groups. Their literature and their prison yard recruiting speeches called for the annihilation of minorities and their goal was an Aryan civilization, with Brotherhood leaders running things.

Clashes between Aryan, black, and Latino gangs had started full-scale riots in prisons from California to Maine. Many inmates, often innocent bystanders trying to avoid prison politics, were killed in these riots and millions of dollars had been spent to repair the facilities. But most of the murder was done without riot. Black prisoners were found hanged in their cells, Latinos were set on fire while they lay in their bunks, whites were found stabbed in showers.

The possibility that the Aryan Brotherhood was now operating among the guards was frightening to Lewis. He knew it was possible and he knew it would have to be stopped.

So Lewis gives the Osborne letters the
highest priority within the circumstances of
his limited resources. He files the Osborne
letters with a note to himself to interview
the inmate on his next trip to Attica during
which he plans to investigate the suspicious
deaths of three inmates. Lewis suspects
guards may have helped smuggle in the poisoned drugs responsible, because following
the death of the first inmate the warden
tightened visiting and mail privileges and
was able to virtually rule out those possibilities as a way the next inmates got the
poisoned drugs. Lewis was a little mad at
himself for not interceding in that investigation, but he had to let the warden try to
solve matters himself. Furthermore, Lewis
was not really responsible for stopping
crime inside the prison. As Inspector General he was primarily concerned with official corruption, e.g., guards' involvement
in the murders.

Lewis retrieves the files when he
notices Osborne's name on an unusual occurrence report; Osborne has been found hanged
in his cell. Preliminary reports indicate
suicide. No one is knocking himself out
investigating the case.

Lewis calls the warden at Attica and
asks if he might be concerned that Osborne
was murdered. The warden is not concerned
at all. He is sure Osborne, whom he de-

scribes as a withdrawn, sullen prisoner, succumbed to lifer's disease. The warden has ordered a review of cell check procedures because Osborne had apparently been overlooked by a guard on a pass through his cell block; perhaps that guard could have saved the inmate's life by cutting him down in time. Perhaps not.

Lewis is not happy with George Prisco's response. The warden of Attica, selected for his toughness, is in charge of the state's most desperate inmates. Not known for his sensitivity to the inmates' problems or fears, he looks at the suicide as available cell space. Lewis thinks the warden would look at an Aryan alliance among his guards as good fraternal fun.

Before the phone is in its cradle, Lewis has decided on his next move. He decides to turn to two men who have helped him solve crimes inside prisons before: Jeff Ford and Dick Walla. Ford is an ex-convict who worked undercover for police and the correction department while doing his time, not so much for the special treatment it got him but because he is that rare individual who enjoys risking his life; he is most alive when at risk. In four years Ford broke up drug-smuggling rings run by guards, solved a murder, and helped convict a warden who was selling weapons and sex to inmates. Walla, on the other hand, is a former guard

who was a member of New York City's elite
prison SWAT team and handled many investigations for Lewis. Walla was assigned to
assist Ford in one of his investigations,
and the two became close friends. Ford, a
tall, black, streetwise adventure lover,
came to look at the middle-aged typical-cop-
type, Walla, as a surrogate father. When
Ford was released from prison, Walla retired
from the department and the two opened a
private detective agency specializing in
undercover operations.

Ford and Walla quickly gained a reputation as a reliable team willing to take
risks and capable of the most sophisticated
assignments. They took on jobs in defense
plants for the FBI, in foreign embassies for
the CIA, and inside prisons all over the
world for correction departments. In one of
their cases Ford obtained a job inside an
aircraft manufacturing plant involved in
building the Stealth Bomber. The FBI and
CIA felt a KGB spy was working inside and
needed to bait him but were afraid to use
one of their own counter-intelligence representatives because if it truly was a KGB
operation in the plant, an agent might be
identified; counter-intelligence is really a
small community.

So Ford and Walla got the assignment.
Ford was given a job in the top secret area
of the plant and Walla was made a security

guard. After a short time Ford's reputation grew, with the help of company technicians, and as the budding genius of the company he was approached by the Russian spy. The bait was offered and taken and the trap was set. The CIA got its man and Ford and Walla's reputation grew.

Lewis shares his suspicions about Attica with Walla and they agree on a plan.

One month after Osborne's "suicide," Jeff Ford is in the back of an ambulance pulling up to the infirmary at Attica Prison, wrapped from head to toe in bandages. The medical charts in his file explain that Ford was seriously burned in an accident at another prison hundreds of miles away. He is being transferred to Attica because the chief doctor there is an expert on treating these injuries. Without much notice, the usually outgoing Ford penetrates the prison.

For six weeks, with the doctors' cooperation, Ford "recovers" in the infirmary. Meanwhile, Walla has entered the prison in the guise of an engineer studying the installation of a completely new plumbing system. He has disguised himself slightly in case he runs into a guard or prisoner he knows from his own days in the department. However he considers this a slight chance because Walla worked almost exclusively for thirty years in prisons in New York City.

Dave Lewis is the only person in the Department of Correction who knows the mission the two detectives are on.

Ford is released from the infirmary and joins the general population. Using his genial personality and a dimwit act which hides his natural con man's brain, he quickly makes friends among the inmates and begins to zero in on Osborne's friends. He learns that they believe Osborne was murdered by the guards. They are not so sure about Osborne's Aryan Nation theory, but they do confirm that the guards are unusually sadistic and clearly racist. Every day Walla finds an excuse to be near Ford so he can get his report. When he leaves the prison each night, Walla reports to Lewis by telephone.

Ford learns that one of the guard ringleaders, Ralph Easter, needs a porter to work in his office. None of the black inmates want the job because they fear Easter. When Ford volunteers, the other inmates tell him he's crazy. However, since he's playing the role of dimwit, he can pretend he doesn't understand their fears.

Ford gets the job and throws himself at Easter's feet. He plays at being too dumb to even understand why the floor has to be swept, and he profusely thanks Easter for every grungy job he gives him. He becomes the butt of Easter's racial jokes and the other guards join in the belief that Ford is some kind of retard.

Soon Ford becomes part of the furniture. The guards talk freely around him and leave important papers concerning the Aryan gang's intelligence reports and meeting summaries around the office. At great risk Walla slips Ford a mini-camera and tape recorder and Ford begins gathering evidence. On more than one occasion a guard suspects Ford is up to something, but the detective's great acting ability always helps him cover up. At one point he even lets a sadistic member of the group beat him over a spilled cup of coffee, but he never drops his act.

When Easter or another guard curses a black man, Ford joins in. When they talk about how great a man Hitler was, Ford jumps up and clicks his heels in the Nazi salute. The guards think Ford is a total imbecile — just what they would expect from a black inmate.

Ford gathers a lot of information about the guards illegal activities but they never mention Osborne. Finally, Lewis decides he must put some pressure on. He tells the Attica warden that he has an undercover agent inside the prison working on the Osborne case. But he does not tell the warden who the agent is or who the leading suspects are.

The warden is furious that Lewis would operate so deviously behind his back. He complains to the Commissioner of Corrections and the Commissioner in turn admonishes Lewis and warns him he better be right about the Aryan gang or his job is at stake.

But Lewis' gamble pays off. One of Easter's thugs, working in the warden's office, overhears a telephone conversation and mentions it during a coffee break in Easter's office. The two guards talk about the murder of Osborne and Easter concedes that he ordered it, and another guard is mentioned as the actual killer. Osborne was killed because he had uncovered a plot by the Aryan guards to smuggle in poisoned drugs to sell to black inmates. The guards would actually make money while achieving their goals of genocide against non-whites. Osborne, apparently tired of waiting for help from Lewis, decided to try to blackmail the guards; it was a fatal decision. Luckily, Ford has been washing the floor at the guard's feet and captures the entire conversation on tape.

Now totally paranoid, the Aryan guards make life hell for the inmates. Cells are repeatedly searched as they hunt for the informant. While Ford remains their mascot, he knows he has to get both his tape and himself out of the jail. His tape recorder and camera are hidden in his mattress when

the guards begin an unannounced search of
his cell block. Ford realizes he needs
Walla immediately, so he decides to flood
his toilet. Using the tape recorder to
stuff up the commode, Ford soon has his way
— the cell block is awash and everyone in
the building calls for a plumber. Walla is
in a maintenance office and realizes the
trouble is coming from Ford's cell block.
He goes with the repair crew, rushing past
them into the cell as soon as he sees it is
Ford's commode. Ford puts on his fool act
and grabs Walla, saying he's the only guy
who can fix the flood.

Walla reaches into the toilet and
retrieves the tape recorder. The cleanup
job has distracted the guards, and when
Walla returns to the cell, Ford tells him
he's got to get out now.

Walla immediately calls Lewis and Ford
is secreted out of the prison the same way
he came in.

In the commissioner's office the next
day, Lewis plays the tape and the arrest of
Easter and his gang is ordered.

Walla and Ford return to their office
in New York to await their next assignment.

```
            WALLA—FORD
Concept for a television series
   based on characters from
       The Inside Man


    By Jerry Schmetterer
```

There is a remarkable man named Jeff
Ford. He is six-foot-seven-inches tall,
looks like Eddie Murphy, and has no peers
among the fast-talking con artists of the
world.

When he was in his early twenties Ford
decided to use his steel nerves and fondness
for danger to become a professional armed
robber. He specialized in sticking up cab
drivers. And he got caught.

He was facing forty years in prison
when a detective named Ed Weiss realized
that Jeff Ford was not your average stick-up
man. He was too smart, too brave, and too
willing to risk his own skin, to let waste
away in prison. The detective thought that
Ford was the right man to do him a very
special favor. He asked Ford to make
friends with an ex-cop in the same cell
block who was being held on charges that he
murdered his wife. This ex-cop was wise to
the ways of the law enforcement. He knew
the cops would only have a solid case
against him if he confessed, and so far that
was something he declined to do. But Weiss

thought that if Jeff Ford could gain the man's confidence then maybe, just maybe, he could get some kind of confession or admission of guilt out of him. And, according to the plan, his confession would be recorded on a secret tape recorder Jeff Ford would be wearing.

In return for this help the detective would pay him $50 a week and try to get Ford's sentence reduced.

Ford was successful. Over a period of weeks, he subtly gained the ex-cop's confidence. Both were avid checkers players and Ford, who considers himself one of the best in the world, let the murder suspect win. He let him win and he let him talk.

Ford pretended he was not the least interested in whatever his checker opponent had to say. Finally, the day came when the killer mentioned why he was in prison. And then Ford began his prodding; off-handedly asking questions until the moment came when the killer told Ford what he had done and bragged about how he would never be convicted. Ford recorded the whole thing and the ex-cop was eventually convicted on murder charges.

Ford got his reward—he was eventually sentenced to only four years in prison—and he got a new start in life. He spent his entire prison stretch working undercover for the Department of Correction helping to nab

crooked and even murderous prison guards,
getting confessions and intelligence and all
the while receiving his $50 a week salary—
plus room and board of course.

During one of his assignments, the
Department of Correction thought that Ford's
life was in extreme danger and so assigned
Correction Officer Dick Walla to keep a
close eye on Ford to make sure that if he
got in trouble he could be rescued.

Dick Walla is a recruiting poster-
image of a cop. He looks, acts, talks, and
thinks exactly like the teachers in the
police academy want their students to be.

To be exact, though, he is actually a
Corrections Officer—prison guard—first
cousin to a cop. He deals with the criminals after the police have put them away.

Walla is as honest as the day is long,
as truthful as he can be without hurting
your feelings, and as dedicated to the basic
values of the Constitution as is humanly
possible. Though a little rumpled and
weighty around the middle as he approaches
fifty, he remains a man's man, father-of-
the-year, no-nonsense guy. This is the guy
you want to be in a foxhole with.

For twenty years Walla worked inside
New York's prisons. He was a member of the
elite CERT unit—Correction Emergency Response Team—called on for help when a jail
was about to explode in riot. If you were a

prisoner in a New York jail and you got out
of hand, you had to deal with Dick Walla and
his CERT buddies. Good luck.

When Walla retired, he, like so many
ex-law-enforcement professionals, opened his
own private detective agency. His desire:
to continue to respond to trouble and solve
problems, this time for big bucks.

He did the usual, hired a secretary,
got an inexpensive office, and hired a bunch
of people he could trust as uniformed security men. His bread and butter would come
from that kind of service. But Walla had a
trick up his sleeve. He knew he would be
able to perform a service offered by no
other agency and perhaps not available anywhere short of government intelligence services. He was bringing Jeff Ford, the inmate who had done so much brave and valuable
undercover work inside New York's prisons,
into his agency.

The two had worked together a few
times and a trusting, father-son type relationship had developed between them. It
would be the Walla-Ford agency.

Walla and Ford became a fearless team.
Ford went undercover in a variety of dis-
guises and characters. One time they busted
a ring of drug-dealing prison guards in
Arizona. Another case found them cleaning
up a notorious welfare hotel. They developed a reputation as a courageous, totally

honest detective team. Their twist: only
Walla is aware that Ford is an undercover
agent. Walla watches everything from a
distance, ready to come to his colleague's
rescue if necessary. Usually they wind up
their cases without even the client knowing
an undercover detective was used. It is
this method that enables Ford to survive.

He has come a long way from his days
as a $50 a week undercover prison inmate,
but without precise planning and split-
second timing—and of course the complete
dedication of Dick Walla—everything could
end for Jeff Ford, very quickly.

THE NOVEL COVERAGE

The following is an example of industry coverage of a novel. Fortunately, as you will read this is excellent coverage and a movie deal was made based on this coverage. Unfortunately, the movie has not been made yet, but we are still working on it.

SAMPLE NOVEL COVERAGE

A MAJOR AGENCY

STORY DEPARTMENT COVERAGE

TITLE: THE BLACK MARIAH

AUTHOR: JAY BONANSINGA

GENRE: SUPERNATURAL SUSPENSE

TYPE/PAGES: NOVEL/463 PGS.

TIME/LOCALE: MID-1990'S/

SOUTHERN AND MIDWEST U.S., LOS ANGELES

SUBMITTED BY: PETER MILLER

STUDIO/NETWORK: N/A

PRODUCTION COMPANY: N/A

PUBLISHER: WARNER BOOKS, INC.

SUBMITTED FOR: PACKAGING

PRODUCER: N/A

DIRECTOR: N/A

TALENT: N/A

PROJECT STATUS: N/A

COVERAGE REQUESTED BY: A MAJOR AGENT

DATE: 5/3/93

READER: A PROFESSIONAL READER AT A MAJOR

AGENCY

CONCEPT:

An African-American truck driver and his
white, female partner go against their better judgement and help out a disturbed man
on the road who claims he's been "cursed."

After failing to save the man's life (moving
along the freeway is the only way to stay
alive), they desperately fight for their own
lives as it seems that they've inherited the
man's ailments. As they search for a spell
to beat the curse they stay alive by continuing to move across the country at any
cost.

<u>SYNOPSIS</u>

THE BLACK MARIAH: By Jay Bonansinga

LUCAS HYDE (late 30's, tall, handsome)
a handsomely well-built African-American
truck driver is driving across rural Georgia
at night with his partner, SOPHIE COHEN
(petit, darkly pretty, Jewish, mid-30's).
They're driving Lucas' state of the art
truck called THE BLACK MARIAH on the front
end of a delivery, and they don't have a job
for their ride back to their homes in Los
Angeles.

It seems to be an ordinary night for
the platonic partners when they hear a desperate voice calling himself MELVILLE BENOIT
(African-American male, late 20's) on the CB
radio Melville tells the pair that the has
been cursed by and elderly, racist witch,
VANESSA DEGEAUX (89), who disapproved of his
engagement to her white niece. His fiancé
has been kidnaped, and not only is he looking for her, he has to keep driving because

if he stops then the curse takes effect. Apparently, when he stops he feels excruciatingly burning pains. Thus, he asks Lucas and Sophie for a ludicrous favor: to fill up his gas tank while both vehicles are still moving. The disbelieving Lucas balks at first but after Sophie plays to weakness for betting and wages $200, he agrees.

They stop and get fuel at a truck stop and there they befriend ANGEL FIGUEROA (a disfigured Hispanic teenager), the only person who will give them a gascan that's perfect for their dangerous stunt. Angel, who has been listening to their bizarre conversation on the CB, offers Lucas his help. They accept. They're amusingly shocked when tens of other truckers cheer them and take bets as the gutsy trio exit the truck stop. Meanwhile, Deputy DELBERT MORRISON (late 20's), a thin, freckled, gung-ho cop, calls his boss SHERIFF DICK BAUM (40's, squat man, racist redneck), and tells him about the stunt that he's heard on the CB that's going to take place. On his way to the scene Baum sees a 1927 Rolls Royce limousine but then it disappears.

With Sophie driving, Angel and Lucas in the trailer manning the gas, and fellow truckers and police looking on, they attempt to pour gas into Melville's tank. They manage to get a little in before he speeds off and they get drenched with gasoline. After

they find Melville on the side of the road a
few miles ahead, they are shocked to see him
combust right in from of their eyes on the
woodside road. Among the fast food contain-
ers and the urine and feces in Melville's
car, Lucas sees and grabs a shriveled, black
hand. As Sheriff Baum approaches, Lucas sees
and scares an elderly chauffeur, who races
back into the woods.

Baum arrests Lucas et. al. But then
releases them, against Delbert's warnings,
because he's too lazy to do all the paper-
work needed for the manslaughter charge he
thinks they're guilty of. Meanwhile, ERIC
KELSINGER (72, bad health, lanky), the
chauffeur Lucas saw and the driver for
Vanessa, has to tell her that he couldn't
find the black hand that Lucas grabbed.
Because she's too weak to talk, Vanessa
expresses her rage at his failure to grab
the talisman, the black hand that spreads
the curse, by typing works onto a screen for
Eric to see.

Angel, in the meantime, goes home to
his UNCLE FLACO (72, tiny Hispanic man,
grey-black hair, deeply lined face), who
keeps a Catholic shrine to his late wife
LOUISA. After the devout Catholic has a
heart seizure, he recovers and notices that
Jesus' left arm in the shrine has turned
black. After Angel tells Flaco of his wild
night and of Lucas' possession of the black

hand, the good-hearted pair take Flaco's bus and try to catch Lucas and Sophie.

While driving west into Illinois, the chain smoking Sophie notices the eerie black hand that Lucas pilfered from Melville's car and asks Lucas to get rid of it. A believer in the unexplained since her friendship began with a hip, mystical RABBI MILO KLEIN in Berkeley, Sophie rightfully believes that the hand is a luck (good or bad?) Charm of some sort. The no-nonsense Lucas, who has recurring nightmares about evil chauffeur drivers, refuses to believe. They pull off and decide to sell the hand to a pawn shop.

After doing some research, Delbert flies to the DeGeaux Estate in Alabama to verify any part of Lucas' and Melville's wild story. There the obese caretaker shows the deputy/amateur detective the DeGeaux family tomb, but they're shocked to find Vanessa's dead father's (MAURICE) tomb semi-open. Delbert's convinced the place is evil when he sees Maurice's right arm missing from his decayed body.

Vanessa bloodily kills a man after he attempts to steal the limo in the same town that she and Eric have followed Lucas to. After Lucas unsuccessfully tries to sell the hand in a small Illinois town, the curse takes its effect on the unsuspecting truck drivers. They double over in excruciating pain, act irrationally, vomit bile and feel as if their stomachs are on fire. They barely make it out on the road after Angel and Flaco show up and help them fill their gas. Just as the late Melville Benoit described, once they get back on the road their ailments go away. They contact Angel and Flaco on the CB and Flaco earns their trust when he tells them that he has a visionary warning about the curse before Angel told him of it. To everybody's chagrin, Lucas loses his temper and throws the black hand out the window.

Speaking in a deliberate, priest-like manner Flaco tells the truckers that he thinks they are in a battle against The Beast (Devil) and that the only way to fight it is with your heart. Lucas and Sohphie need gas so they stop and Lucas sprints to fill the tank. The pain is worse and sparks and smoke emanates from the large trucker. With Angel's help they fill the tank but not before the gas station catches on fire and explodes. They get back on the highway but Lucas' hands are burned, his temples pound, and his lungs are "roasted." Taking illegal pills to kill the pain and stay awake, Lucas and Sophie continue driving.

Flaco and Angel put gas into a can and offer the couple to repeat their earlier stunt of gassing up while both vehicles move. The couple agree to it, but when Angel slips and fall on the gas, Lucas grabs him

and saves his life. However, by touching the
cursed one - Lucas - Angel is now cursed
himself.

Sheriff Baum, in the meantime, falsely
believes that Lucas and Sophie are guilty of
all the strange happenings in the last few
days: the vandalized DeGeaux tomb,
Melville's death, the gas station exploding.
Baum and the federal police track down The
Black Mariah and the long bus trailing it.
Baum tells them over his P.A. system that
they're under arrest and need to pull over.
Lucas tries to tell the cop that he can't
stop.

Baum calls Lucas a racist slur and
gives way to the Feds. Flaco, however, uses
his bus as interference and bumps the Fed's
car when they start shooting bullets at the
cursed trio. This MAD MAX scenario continues
until Lucas sees a road block ahead that he
goes right through. Before the Feds rain
down bullets on Flaco and kill him, he
crashed into them and the two cars explode.
The Black Mariah jackknifes and crashes, and
the other police cars are also damaged. The
limo carrying Eric and Vanessa is the final
part of this violent pileup; Eric is killed
while Vanessa survives.

Lucas, Sophie, and Angel leave their
truck behind, steal Baum's damaged police
car, and keep moving westward. Though she is
an invalid and her driver is dead, Vanessa

is empowered by the Devil's hate and continues to drive after Lucas et. al. To torment
them. Convinced that they have to find a
cure for their ailment, Sophie uses the car
phone and calls Rabbi Klein in Berkeley for
advice. He is supportive and tells them
about the vast resources of Jewish mysticism
that he's drawing on for his advice. He
tells them that a sacrifice is usually necessary to rid oneself of an evil curse.

A ghost in the demonic limo takes on
all forms of beings as it taps into the
fears of each cursed person. Then it magi-
cally disappears. As they cross from Mis-
souri to Kansas they decide to try and hop
into a moving train while driving the cop
car. They drop Angel off at a rural train
station and he kidnaps the good-natured
conductor of a freight train and has him
take a specific route that he and Lucas
planned on. When they get there Lucas and
Sophie dangerously, yet successfully, jump
aboard. After Lucas and Sophie finally admit
that they're attracted to each other, Lucas
gives her some pills to sleep on.

Angel, who's been keeping the conductor honest by putting a shotgun in his back,
alerts Lucas to the fact that Vanessa is
driving alongside the train. Lucas, tired of
running his whole life and willing to make
the <u>sacrifice</u> of his life to rid the curse,
jumps into the caboose car and separates it

from the rest of the train. He's inviting
the demonic old woman to take him on. True
to form, she inexplicably jumps into the
slowing down caboose and physically torments
him. While writhing from pain he wakes up
and finds himself mysteriously lying in a
rural southern field at night. There the
ghost of MAURICE DEGEAUX (Vanessa's father)
appears and beats Vanessa like he did on the
day that he paralyzed her for kissing a
little black boy. Apparently, Vanessa torments African-American males to this day for
this reason.

Unlike the little boy that day, Lucas
does not run away. Instead, he walks up to
the ghost and screams at him to leave
Vanessa alone and to go away. This breaks
the curse and the ghost goes away. Lucas
wakes up and finds himself in the burning
caboose. Lucas, an ex-football player, ath-
letically jumps out of the caboose. Just as
it burst into flames, he sees a finally
happy Vanessa (or possibly her ghost) danc-
ing gaily on it. He lands hard on the ground
but is alright. His hands and wounds are
healed. Angel and Sophie stop the train and
Lucas and Sophie embrace lovingly.

Angel, Sophie, and Lucas then turn
themselves into the Colorado state authorities and with a plea bargaining and a willingness to forget their outrageous story
they were spared doing any prison time. They

settle in Nevada where they have a son
(which they name Flaco) and get married.
They own a gas station which employs Angel
and both Lucas and Sophie live happily in
their new home with their newfound peace of
mind. Lucas has finally stopped running.

<u>EVALUATION</u>

THE BLACK MARIAH: By Jay Bonansinga
COMMENTS: This novel entitled THE BLACK
MARIAH reads like the truck it is named
after. Once it gets going it's hard to stop,
as this action-packed suspense story lumbers
along with increasing speed and thrills. It
has that rare distinction of possessing both
lots of quick-paced, violent action and
compelling subplots involving deeply tex-
tured characters.

These are characters that the reader
can sink his/her teeth into; they are viv-
idly - yet concisely - drawn, and hero and
villain alike has a depth and three-dimen-
sionality that is all-too-rare in fiction.
Much of the characters' mettle, courage,
hopes and, especially fears are illustrated
through dialogue that is always believable
and further serves to heighten the tension.

Even at 463 pages, this story reads
like a taut thriller that highly entertains
while reflecting upon the different faced of
America. Indeed, there is a large multi
cultural theme present, with the three main

protagonists (one disfigured Hispanic, one
African-American male, one Jewish woman)
representing the U.S. diversity as much as
the story's various settings and terrains
(from L.A. to rural Georgia do. All of this
occurs in a scenario which contains a mixture of elements that recalls Spielberg's
DUEL and more recently, THE ROAD WARRIOR.

  Furthermore, THE BLACK MARIAH works on
many levels. While the action entertains,
the more esoteric issues of responsibility,
conquering one's own fears, and peace of
mind are explored. And while the novel's
bizarre denouement depicting the disabled
white woman tormenting Lucas stretches plau-
sibility and borders on parody, there is
plenty of taut dramatic tension to make a
compelling drama with definite cinematic
possibilities.

   EXCELLENT GOOD FAIR PASS

DIALOGUE X.....X

CHARACTERIZATION X.....X

PLOT LINE X.....X

STORY STRUCTURE X.....X

RECOMMEND___X___   CONSIDER_____
PASS_____

KEY LEADS

THE BLACK MARIAH: By Jay Bonansinga

LUCAS HYDE - late 30's, goatee, handsome
African-American male, big man, a truck
driver with a good heart, intelligent, near-
ing bankruptcy, expert on black R&B music,
attracted to his female, Jewish partner.

SOPHIE COHEN - Jewish, liberal, woman, mid-
30's, pretty, dark hair, brown eyes, from
rich parents, college educated, independent,
tomboyish, smart.

MELVILLE BENOIT - late 20's, African-American who's been cursed to keep moving or die,
desperate, fell in love with white girl
whose racist aunt put curse on him

VANESSA DEGEAUX - a racist witch (literally), 89, paralyzed from abuse from her
Satan worshiping father, puts curse on
Melville and Lucas, puts curse on black men,
speaks with a CompuTalk machine while being
chauffeured around in an old limousine,
deformed looking

SHERIFF DICK BAUM - squat little man, no
neck, square jawed redneck, mid 40's, chews
tobacco, Sheriff of Pennington County gets
killed when his roadblock of Lucas' runaway
truck goes awry.

ANGEL FIGUEROA - Hispanic, works at a truck
stop, 19, has deformed face from a congeni-
tal birth defect, has intelligence and passion, abused by most because of his face,
Lucas and Sophie befriend him.

Rave Reviews for *Get Published! Get Produced!*

"Getting published is a shade more difficult than walking on water. In *Get Published! Get Produced!* Peter Miller brings the boat."
JAY BARBREE—*Moon Shot; A Journey Through Time; The Complete History Of Mars*

"Peter Miller runs with the wolves, he swims with the sharks—hell, he's the biggest, baddest fish in the ocean—but what is most important, he always-always-always knows what's best for his clients. He's the Jake Lamotta of literary managers; he takes a licking and keeps on ticking. His connections are innumerable, but his energy is far greater. Pay close attention to this guy. His riffs are pure gold."
JAY BONANSINGA—*The Killer's Game; The Black Mariah; Sick*

"There's no better literary representative, anywhere, than Peter Miller. I have found him to be very enterprising, extremely knowledgeable, and tireless in his representation of me. His book is an invaluable resource in guiding any author's career."
VINCENT BUGLIOSI—*Helter Skelter; And The Sea Will Tell; Outrage*

"This book is a must for anyone who has ever been rejected by an agent or a publisher. Do yourself a very big favor and read it!"
ANN BENSON—*The Plague Tales*

"Peter Miller's fast, he's good, he's determined, he's tireless, he knows the business like Casanova knew his moves, and he really cares. Read *Get Published! Get Produced!* and learn from the Master."
DR. SUSAN BLOCK—*The 10 Commandments Of Pleasure; Being A Woman; Advertising For Love*

"Peter Miller is the best friend an aspiring writer ever had. My novel, *Bohemian Heart*, was rejected by seven agents and 38 publishers before he sold it to a publisher who had already rejected it twice. He is the absolute best at what he does.
JAMES DALESSANDRO—*Bohemian Heart*

"Peter Miller read my book *Miss Fourth Of July, Goodbye* and within three weeks sold it to Disney. Within a year Disney made my book into a film nominated for four Emmy Awards. This is a kind of miracle in the book publishing and movie business—and the kind of accomplishment Peter Miller is famous for. He's absolutely the best."
CHRISTOPHER G. JANUS—*Miss Fourth Of July Goodbye; Search For Peking Man; Angel On My Shoulder*

"Peter Miller has managed my career from my first novel to my first bestseller (and second and third!). He knows publishing from all the angles and every genre, and he can even handle the complexities of Hollywood. I wouldn't trust anyone else to give me guidance, and I recommend Peter's advice for anyone who intends to be a professional writer."
SUSAN WRIGHT—*The History Of Mars, Area 51; Four Star Trek Novelizations*

"No one understands the 'ins and outs' of the publishing business better then Peter Miller. If he can't make the deal, it can't be made. A literary lion, for sure."
MICHAEL C. EBERHARDT—*Body Of Crime; Against The Law, The Fifth Canon*

"There's no one quite like Peter Miller when it comes to the publishing business. He's a strong willed character with a heart of gold who always gets the best deals for his clients. Peter plays the game to perfection."
WENSLEY CLARKSON—*Deadly Seduction; Quentin Tarantino*

(continued on next page)

"Peter Miller is a lion among literary representatives. He's without question the manager to have in your corner with his sheer tenacity, super contacts and clear vision to carry you through to that final bell of publication."
JOHN GLATT —*River Phoenix; The Chieftains; Holy Killers*

'This book should be every aspiring writer's bible! Within six months of reading it, I received a contract for my first book, all because of Peter Miller. Peter thrives on the chaos of the literary and film indistry and has boundless energy and passion that produces wins for those he represents! As agents go, he's untouvhable . . . undoubtedly the *king* of deal makers!"
TAMMY L. KLING—*Family Secrets*

"Peter Miller is one tenacious bulldog of a literary manager. He <u>never</u> gives up. In a business of a million "nos," Peter Miller always manages to find that "yes." He is a true artist of the deal."
WILLIAM STADIEM—*Marilyn Monroe Confidential; Lullaby And Good Night; Madame 90210*

"Every writer needs a champion to negotiate value in the marketplace. To say that Peter Miller knows how to make deals is like saying he knows how to put his shoes on in the morning. The deals are out there, and the man knows how to finesse them, and that's that. But he is so much more. Peter demands a writer's best work—he will represent nothing less. When he gets a piece of work that lives and sings, Peter gets excited. He shouts and stamps and waves the gauntlet, and there is not a better champion any writer could have."
CHRIS ROGERS—*Bitch Quotient*

"Peter Miller delivers. I have worked with a variety of literary agents and managers throughout my publishing and Hollywood career, but Peter's tenacity, intuition and pure chutzpa is without equal. In the parlance of complexity thinking, he's a highly successful self-organizing autonomous agent, operating at the edge of chaos, and open to the adjacent possibilities that emerge."
RON SCHULTZ—*Unconventional Wisdom: Twelve Remarkable Innovators Tell How Intuition Can Revolutionize Decision Making; Open Boundaries: Putting Complexity And Innovation To Work, Cashing Out* (with Jim Arkebauer)

"Peter Miller is a good talker. But, hey, lots of agents are good talkers. So what makes Peter Miller better than all those other ragents? Here's a little secret: Peter Miller is also a good listener. Peter really listens to what people need . . . and then he figures out a way to make it happen. That's his secret weapon."
JOAN DETZ—*How To Write & Give A Speech; You Mean I Have To Stand Up And Say Something; Can You Say A Few Words?*

"Peter Miller is a Merlin among agents. he will work magic with your career, with your projects and with your success. you can struggle for years to try to discover the writer you are, or you can allow Peter to help you actualize all facets of the creative and successful writer hiding within you and launch that fully realized creative force into the marketplace with a big splash—I cannot think of any greater gift to one who feels compelled to answer the call of writing."
RONNIE EDELL, PH.D.—*How To Save Your Marriage From An Affair; The Sexually Satisfied Woman: The Five Steps Program For Getting Everything You Want In Bed*

"I have never known a more dedicated person. If the ice you give him is good enough, Peter Miller could sell it to Eskimos. Every day of his life he says something nice about me to somebody in New York or Hollywood. What more could a writer ask for than that?"
CHRISTOPHER COOK GILMORE—*Atlantic City Proof; The Bad Room; Hemingway*

"Peter Miller has managed my career from its start. Through the sale of seven novels to major publishers over as many years. I have learned to trust and depend on him. He's a caring man in a demanding business, tending clients large and small."
JOHN S. McCORD—*Walking Hawk; The Baynes Clan Series* (six novel series)